ROOTS AND RESILIENCE

ROOTS AND RESILIENCE

California Ranchers in Their Own Words

EDITED BY SUSAN EDINGER MARSHALL,
DAN MACON, GRANT SCOTT-GOFORTH,
AND MICHAEL DELBAR

FOREWORD BY VALERIE ELDER

UNIVERSITY OF NEVADA PRESS | *Reno & Las Vegas*

University of Nevada Press | Reno, Nevada 89557 USA
www.unpress.nevada.edu

Manufactured in the United States of America
FIRST PRINTING
Cover design by Louise OFarrell.
Cover photographs © iStock.com/Mycan (front),
iStock.com/Instants (back)

Library of Congress Cataloging-in-Publication Data
Names: Marshall, Susan Edinger, 1958- editor.
Title: Roots and resilience : California ranchers in their own words /
   [edited by] Susan Edinger Marshall, Valerie Elder, Daniel K. Macon,
   Grant Scott-Godforth, Michael Delbar.
Other titles: California ranchers in their own words
Description: Reno, Nevada : University of Nevada Press, [2024] |
   Includes bibliographical references. | Summary: "An edited collec-
   tion of essays and poems, *Roots and Resilience* provides a first-hand
   account of ranching and ranchers in California. Reflected in these
   essays and poems are the perspectives of Indigenous, Mexican-
   American, Basque, and Euro-American ranchers alike, with a
   predominance of contributions coming from women. Through this
   diversity of perspectives, the complexity of issues faced by contemporary ranchers in the American West is given voice."— Provided by
   publisher.
Identifiers: LCCN 2024004431 | ISBN 9781647791612 (paper) | ISBN
   9781647791629 (ebook)
Subjects: LCSH: Ranching—California—Anecdotes. | Ranching—
   California—Poetry. | Ranch life—California—Anecdotes. | Ranch
   life—California—Poetry. | Ranchers—California—Anecdotes. |
   Ranchers—California—Poetry. | LCGFT: Anecdotes. | Poetry.
Classification: LCC F866.2 .R66 2024 | DDC 979.4/008863—dc23/
   eng/20240403

LC record available at https://lccn.loc.gov/2024004431
ISBN 978-1-64779-161-2 (paper)
ISBN 978-1-64779-162-9 (ebook)
LCCN: 2024004431

The paper used in this book meets the requirements of American
National Standard for Information Sciences—Permanence of Paper
for Printed Library Materials, ANSI/NISO Z39.48–1992 (R2002).

For Phil Reed Ogden, who told us to consider one ranch at a time

Contents

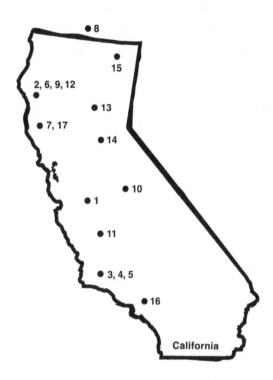

Ranch Locations of Contributing Authors

1. Soares, DiGiovanni (Merced Co.)
2. Moore et al. (Humboldt Co.)
3. Schley (Santa Barbara Co.)
4. Goforth Doiron (Santa Barbara Co.)
5. Gibford (Santa Barbara Co.)
6. Cottrell (Humboldt Co.)
7. Sagehorn Russell (Mendocino Co.)
8. Sampert Scribner (Jackson Co.)
9. Giacomini (Humboldt Co.)
10. Bernikoff (Mariposa Co.)
11. Varian (Monterey Co.)
12. Stansberry (Humboldt Co.)
13. Daley (Butte Co.)
14. Macon (Placer Co.)
15. DeForest (Modoc Co.)
16. Williams (Los Angeles Co.)
17. Delbar Moore (Mendocino Co.)

Foreword

VALERIE ELDER

This book is a collection of stories, poems, and musings by ranchers. Most take a memoir form. From my perspective as a resource manager, I know that it's, of course, impossible to tell the story of ranching in California without focusing on the people. The land has its own tale to tell—one connected to time, humanity, plants and animals, weather, geography, and traditions unique to each place—and these writers know it well. As you read on, perhaps starting to feel these associations too, you will sense how the land becomes an extension of self, becomes a "sense of place."

For these writers, their furrowed brow is akin to the ridgelines of their land, and their knowledge of the seasons, the plants, soils, and slopes is gleaned from years spent in the hills, among the trees, and along the streams. Some of them may not learn from generations of family lore but rather by listening to their neighbors and to the land itself. Regardless of how they get their knowledge, the land becomes them, the roads their wrinkles, a mountain saddle their broad shoulders.

Their ranches are, of course, often family businesses. Families are beautiful and messy. It's not easy to work together and to live together. It's challenging, too, to be part of a multigenerational ranching family because the values and ideas that everyone has in common wane. Ranchers may feel incredibly vulnerable about sharing such private challenges, as well as about sharing their connection to the land and the stories that are extensions of themselves. They are opening themselves—the good and the bad—to the eyes of others.

I am therefore especially grateful to the brave ones who have shared their words here. If you are a rancher reading this, I encourage you to scribble your own notes and to pass them on to others one day, when you feel brave. Maybe you will share them with your grandkids or even with your own legislature. Your story matters. It is embedded in the landscape, but few can read the landscape's language without your help.

Although they are often lumped into narrow categories, landowners, ranchers, farmers, and others who make their livelihood on the land are some of the most diverse, creative, and conservation-minded people

I know. Their diversity is evident in these stories of roots and resilience, and their words motivate me to seek common ground across fence lines on behalf of land stewardship and conservation. I think a critical piece of this lies in recognizing the sense of place and ethics of landowners and ranchers. We can accomplish more by working together than we can by fighting against each other, while human and environmental forces continue to shape our landscapes.

One of the complexities of managing an entire ecosystem is contending with the diverse lifestyles, emotions, and relationships associated with the people who make use of the land. When we go about living our own lives, it's easy to blame others for the challenges surrounding us. I ask us, instead, to act responsibly in our actions as humans and to seek to work together to accomplish broader goals for maintaining this open-space ecosystem. We should think about the big picture, the landscape-level view: what we see from an airplane window, or across the West, or throughout the entire United States. We should consider all the lives in these places, both human and wild. At the same time, we should consider the small scale, the lives and goals of people within the bounds of their own land, the law, and the politics of ranching in California.

Of course it's challenging to swallow viewpoints that contrast with your own. As a resource professional, I find it hard sometimes to listen to local expertise when I have such in-depth training. It's similarly hard for landowners who know their land so well: why should they listen to new ideas when they know what works and which regulations limit their creativity in accomplishing their goals? Moving forward, however, depends on everyone sharing knowledge and listening to each other's stories.

I hope that something in this collection speaks to you, knowing that what pulls each of us may be a little different. This collection reflects this variation, but I know there are stories left untold. I encourage you to breathe in these perspectives, some smooth and seasoned like a leather saddle, others young, sprouting leaves in the warmth of the spring sun. You won't agree with everything—none of us will—and from that we will all learn something. We can, however, share our appreciation of the land, of family, of our struggles . . . of roots and resilience.

Preface

SUSAN EDINGER MARSHALL

After Mrs. Stafford's horse property next door had been obliterated by the construction of the Pomona Freeway, I would watch charros make their way slowly up a newly extended Landis View Lane. The charros' cobbled-together corrals and shelters of corrugated metal were clustered together downslope from where I grew up, on land overlooking the Rio Hondo. Their way out of the river bottom, up Muscatel Avenue, had been cut off by eight lanes of noisy traffic. The Mexican American rider's horse lightly clopped along the residential street. The charro wore his broad-brimmed hat with the chin strap tight under his lower lip.

My childhood home was a one-acre property that my mom put a hold on by giving the previous owner a $20 bill until she could discuss the purchase with my dad. My grandparents raised poultry, a garden, and fruit trees there, and our neighbors kept livestock before the freeway and housing developments came. What may be surprising is that this property, which is close to the original Mission San Gabriel Arcángel site in Indigenous Tongva territory, is only about ten miles due east of Los Angeles City Hall, as the crow flies.

We urban Californians are not so far removed from rural traditions as the mass media might lead some to believe. I get choked up when I watch the equestrian units prance down Colorado Boulevard during the Rose Parade. We mourn the vacant lots, sage scrub, chaparral, oak woodlands, and grasslands that got converted to tract homes, tilt-up industrial parks, shopping centers, and other uses.

But the open lands and the people who live and work on them are out there still. In our most populous state of 39 million souls, about 60 percent of the state's acreage is considered varied rangeland, with about 40 percent managed for grazing domestic livestock. In this collection of essays and poems, we have invited rangeland stewards in the Golden State to share their stories with like-minded people who appreciate productive open spaces and wildlife habitats that remain intact. The urban majority relishes California's wide-open landscapes, even if we don't understand the whole story of how these rangelands have escaped the developers' heavy equipment.

Roots and Resilience gives voice to California's Indigenous and immigrant ranchers, of varying land tenure and region. The stories and poems were written by everyone from transplanted suburbanites to seventh-generation heirs. The authors ruminate on the holiness of landscapes, mourn for those who have died but whose presence is still sensed, and express the delight of sharing nature with grandkids. Women writers have contributed most of these pieces. Their stories and poems reflect California's rich Indigenous, Mexican American, Basque, and other Euro-American traditions.

Young adults, elders, and rural neighbors from all over the state have written these essays and poems. They recount hard work in adverse weather conditions, the unforgiving nature of the elements, and the sounds and smells of a special place. They probe different perspectives with regard to predators and livestock. And, as in Dave Daley's piece, they drag us through the outright anger and anguish of a place destroyed by preventable wildfire. The simple message of this book is that things may be complicated, but the long-term and observant tenants of a place know it intimately and can best predict what will happen when many moving parts are stressed by drought, fire, or mismanagement.

The inspiration for *Roots and Resilience* came from a collection titled *Home Land: Ranching and a West That Works*, edited by Laura Pritchett, Richard L. Knight, and Jeff Lee. I have used *Home Land* for more than a decade in my introductory Rangeland Resource Science class at Cal Poly Humboldt. I am repeatedly surprised by the heartfelt written responses from students based on prompts for each piece in the *Home Land* collection. My students regard this book with great affection for its humanity, stories of collaboration and frustration, and deep yearning for a place that can be called home. A few students have a familial ranching connection in the western United States or in Mexico, but many do not. These young adults write about their own hard-working family members, their own care for animals, and the wide-open landscapes they treasure. They desire a connection to the earth and the ecosystem services it provides—directly and vicariously.

Roots and Resilience will give future students a chance to read California stories. We invite you also to "listen" to the tales to learn more about the wild places in California that are called working landscapes. And we ask you for a favor: if you know a young person or a non-traditional student who wants to work and live on our rangelands, ask them to consider a career as a rangeland management specialist. The U.S. Forest

Service, Natural Resources Conservation Service, Bureau of Indian Affairs, and Bureau of Land Management are some of the organizations that seek to hire people for this position. Universities offer coursework and degrees in rangeland resource science and rangeland ecology and management; please see rangelands.org for more information. Be sure to advise these prospective students that when they go in to the field, they will be rewarded if they listen carefully and patiently to those who have deep roots in these open spaces and lifetimes of resilience.

ROOTS AND RESILIENCE

ROOTS

There are few areas of the planet so mythologized as the American West. It was here long before any humans set foot on the land, long before Indigenous peoples or European settlers arrived. Although the land has been here forever, the "Roots" written about in this collection are relatively recent. But they make up part of the storied landscape of California's rangelands, with all their bumps in the road included. These pieces look back at the families, communities, and businesses whose complicated relationships with the forests, mountains, plains, rivers, animals—wild and domesticated—and each other have led up to this point in our human history.

Talbott Sheep Company

MIA ARTADI DIGIOVANNI, GIANNA ARTADI DIGIOVANNI,
BIANCA ARTADI SHAPERO, AND TRISTAN TALBOTT SOARES

The story of Talbott Sheep Company is many things. Of course, it is a story of a sheep business that has survived more than one hundred years. But it is so much more than that. It is a story of culture and history. It is a story of hardworking Basque sheepmen and strong Basque women. It is a story of good and bad times, of perseverance and grit. A story of innovation and adaptation. But most of all, it is the story of our family. We grew up hearing this story, and for all our lives, we've watched our grandparents, Aitachi and Amachi, live and breathe the sheep industry. Putting their story, our story, on paper has been a privilege and an honor.

Talbott Sheep Company is a 101-year-old commercial sheep business, a lifeline for Basque sheepherders who immigrated to the United States for a better life. To understand the story of Talbott Sheep Co., you need to understand the story of two different families—the Iribarrens and the Artadis. Thomas Iribarren immigrated to the United States in 1921 from Elizondo (Navarre province), Spain, and worked as a herder for a sheepman in Lost Hills, California. He eventually built his own sheep business, married Marie Jeanne Eyherabide in Bakersfield, and raised his daughters, Teresa and Dolores, around the sheep. This is where Teresa's passion for sheep began.

The Artadis are a slightly different story. Ramon Artadi immigrated to the United States in 1906 from near Gernika (or Guernica) in the Bizkaia (or Biscay) province, Spain, when he was eleven years old, along with his father, Jose Artadi. They both worked as sheepherders for a man named James Talbott in Nevada. After a few years, Jose decided it was time for him to go back to Spain. Ramon didn't wish to return.

Jose went to Mrs. Talbott and asked her in these words, now famous in our family: "Will you have him?" Mrs. Talbott turned to Jose, smiled, and said, "Yes, we will have him."

The Talbotts adopted Ramon, he changed his name to Ramon Artadi Talbott, and he never saw his father again. Three generations later, every member of our family still carries Artadi as a middle name.

Ramon eventually got a job working for Tryon and McKendry Wool Company near Klamath, California. One day, he was out moving sheep in terribly rough weather, and a car pulled up with a man in the back seat. The man asked, "Whom do these sheep belong to?"

Ramon responded, not knowing who the man was: "They belong to Tryon and McKendry."

Mr. Tryon was the man in the car. He gained a lot of respect for Ramon. "Anyone that's going to be out in weather like that moving sheep for another man has got to be a pretty square guy," he said.

Ramon was offered a new position with the wool company in Stockton, California. Stockton was a hub for the Central Valley sheep industry and for Basques. His job was to visit sheep producers who were being financed by Tryon and to count the sheep, to assess Tryon's assets. At that time, sheep outfits were financed by the wool companies, not by banks. Ramon carried a little pink book around with him for his counts and came to be known by many as "Pink Book."

Ramon started Talbott Sheep Co. in Stockton in 1920. During this time, he met Elena Celayeta. They married in 1929 and moved to Los Banos, California, in 1931. Ramon and Elena had two sons, James "Jim" Artadi Talbott (named after James Talbott, Ramon's adoptive father), who was born in 1933, and Raymond "Ray" Artadi Talbott (named after Ramon), who was born in 1938. The boys grew up in the business, and when their father suddenly passed away in 1956, when Ray was a senior in high school, the brothers took over and ran Talbott Sheep Co. together. While the brothers managed the sheep, their mother, Elena, managed the books.

Elena had left school at age twelve to work to help her family. As an adult, she returned to school, attending night classes, and graduated from high school in the same year as her son Ray. She was very well read, spoke five languages, and was involved in many local organizations. She was always ready to help those in her community, helping many Basques with the paperwork necessary to achieve American citizenship.

Our Aitachi (grandfather), Ray Artadi Talbott, attended the University of California, Davis, for two years while working with the business.

He eventually decided he needed to focus on the business more and returned to the ranch full-time. He also served in the National Guard for a few years. He met Teresa Iribarren at the Reno Basque Picnic, and they were married in 1965. After their wedding, Thomas Iribarren, Teresa's father, retired and sold his business to Talbott Sheep Co., uniting their herds and their families. To this day, we still use some of Thomas's original brands.

Ray and Teresa had two daughters, Michelle and Andrée, who were raised around the sheep, but both followed in their mother's footsteps and became nurses. When Talbott Sheep Co. bought the sheep from Thomas, they also gained one of his Basque herders, Santiago. Santiago worked for Talbott Sheep Co. until he retired. Ray Bilbao "Quinientos" was another significant herder. Quinientos came to Stockton from Reno with Ramon and worked for Ramon from the start. He was very close with the Talbott Family until he passed.

In the 1980s, due to pressing economic concerns, Ray and Jim had to sell the sheep. During this difficult time, Ray always knew he would get back into the industry. He built back little by little, traded old ewes, and eventually got into the sheep business on his own. He credits Teresa for keeping their affairs together during this period, as she had an off-farm job that provided stability. After Elena passed, Teresa "managed the books," as she called it. In reality, she managed much more than that. She dove in and, together with Ray's help, soon became responsible for the banking, insurance, payroll, H-2A visa program, all the things that keep a business like ours going. She did so while working full-time as a school nurse and raising their two daughters. This story is not uncommon: sheepwomen have been helping to manage their family businesses from behind the scenes for generations, often without the recognition they deserve.

Ray passed away in August of 2022. If you are in the sheep industry in most of the western United States, you have likely heard about Ray Talbott. He served on many different boards for industry organizations throughout his life, including the California Wool Growers Association (CWGA) and the Western Range Association (WRA), and he received the Master Shepherd Award from the CWGA in honor of his time and service to the industry. He was a historian of the industry and a wise sheepman who was looked to for advice and guidance by others for many decades.

Ray was a quiet man. He always told us grandkids that we have two ears and one mouth for a reason: that is, to listen twice as much as we speak. But anyone who attended a sheep ranchers' conference or who met with Ray knew that when he spoke, the room went silent to listen to what he had to say. He spoke wisely and wasn't afraid to challenge an idea or opinion. The kind of respect Ray got from his listeners came from knowing that he had spent years paying attention and learning about what was going on around him, another piece of advice he often gave to his grandkids.

Today Talbott Sheep Co. is a meat and wool production outfit. We raise Rambouillet sheep, focusing on the best practices available to ensure the best quality of lamb and wool. Our sheep spend their falls and winters in Los Banos, in the heart of the Central Valley, just as they have since 1931 when Ramon and Elena moved the sheep and their family to town. The only difference is that they spend their springs and summers grazing in the Sierra Nevada. In 2020 Talbott Sheep Company joined Shaniko Wool Company as a Responsible-Wool-Standard-certified ranch. This recent partnership has allowed us to sell our wool into a more active market. Now, a few years later, we have added a second certification, NATIVARegen, to our operation. These third-party, audited certifications are incredibly rigorous and assure brands that we follow the highest standards of care for our employees, our livestock, and our grazing lands.

Although our sheep were originally herded by Basque shepherds, today our bands are herded by H-2A Peruvian shepherds who are experts in their trade. Sheep companies would not exist without the expert care of these herders. They are a crucial part of the industry, as is the H-2A worker program. These men are very special to our family, and many have worked with us for decades. They are truly invaluable and part of the heart of our operation.

While our sheep are grazing the Sierra Nevada, they are also providing wildfire fuel reduction, and in some areas, they are working to maintain native vegetation species that are monitored by the U.S. Forest Service. The sheep and the land have a symbiotic relationship. The healthier the soils, the more nutritious the feed is for our sheep, the more efficiently they graze, and the more impact they have on helping to stimulate healthy plant growth and to diminish wildfire fuel.

In 2014, Ray and Teresa's daughter Andrée, after twenty-nine years working as a nurse for Valley Children's Hospital, decided it was time for a change: She came back to the sheep industry, and she began growing

Star Creek Land Stewards Inc. (SCLS) into the company it is today. SCLS is a sheep and goat wildfire-fuels-reduction grazing company. Andrée now heads the company and serves on many of the same boards that her father served on, including the CWGA (the oldest agricultural organization in the state), and she is the first woman to serve on the board of the WRA.

This evolution created a grand opportunity for Andrée's daughter, Bianca, who, like her Amachi Teresa, has a grand passion for this industry and the animals. Bianca works as the Project Manager for SCLS and is also heavily involved with continuing the work of Talbott Sheep Co.

Our family has a long tradition of strong women guiding our businesses forward. SCLS is effective in what it does because of the tradition, experience, Basque culture, and passion we all bring to the company. Andrée, Bianca, and Emilio Huarte Jr. lead the company. Emilio's father, Emilio Sr., immigrated to the United States from Ardaiz, Navarre, Spain, in 1958 at the age of twenty-one. He began working for Talbott Sheep Co. in 1959. Emilio was the foreman for Ray for many years, and Emilio Jr. and his siblings were all raised around the sheep business and the Talbott family. Emilio Jr. always had an immense passion for the industry and eventually took on the role of foreman at Talbott Sheep Co., just as his father had. Emilio Jr. brought the concept of SCLS to Andrée in 2013 and currently serves as foreman for both Talbott Sheep Co. and SCLS. The knowledge he has from years of listening to old sheepmen tell him secrets of the trade, mistakes to avoid, and those to learn from, along with his overall experience, have made him, his father, and their families not only crucial parts of our businesses but also part of our family.

SCLS specifically focuses on wildfire-fuels-reduction grazing with sheep and goats, on land restoration, and on vegetation management. Compared with a typical sheep outfit, we require more attentiveness from our herders, as we put our animals and herders in urban settings, exposing them to many different types of risks. But on the ground level, we are using the same practices our great-grandparents used when they began raising sheep in the United States over one hundred years ago. It is a business that is being more commonly utilized as states like California learn about the importance of tending to the land. We can no longer allow our state to neglect its public lands, leaving them at risk to become completely overgrown, overtaken by invasive species and brush, and, ultimately, an imminent threat for fueling wildfires. Utilizing a service like what we provide not only helps to protect the land from disasters such as

wildfires, but it also uses grazing animals that mimic the native herd species that used to roam the land. This grazing system keeps native grasses
at healthy levels, allowing them to thrive. It manages invasive species,
disturbs the soils to stimulate root growth, and creates natural fertiliz-
ers that provide the soils with a healthy, strong microbiome. Grazing is
one of a few healthy options for managing our lands, along with other
natural practices, and it is what sheep outfits have been doing across the
western United States for centuries. SCLS has simply pivoted and found
a new way to apply them to the needs of California today.

Today some might look at a legacy like ours and think that it's easy
because it's a family business, and we already have the know-how to run
a sheep outfit. But the sheep business is anything but easy. It is extraordi-
narily complex and never dull. It is an industry that has been challenged
to fail for decades. The market for lamb and wool has been on a decline
since the late 1970s, when lamb began to be imported from other coun-
tries. The wool market followed a similar trend. Today, fortunately, there
are more niche markets in search of quality companies that are providing a superior product. What is truly impressive is that we have survived.
It is a testament to our work that a multigenerational company, threatened by economic, financial, personal, and environmental challenges,
has adapted time and time again. We have continued to change and will
continue to do so.

When Bianca was no more than eight years old, her little brother,
Tristan, drew a picture of the two of them with the sheep and shared it
with our Aitachi Ray, saying, "Look Tachi, this is going to be Bianca and
me when we're grown up and running the sheep!"

It was a dream for us as kids. Aitachi Ray looked back at us and
said, "The sheep industry will be gone by the time you're adults," and he
turned away. That was the opinion of most sheepmen at that time. It's the
opinion of many sheepmen even today. Faced with more and more challenges regarding the reliability of labor, and the diminishing markets for
American wool and lamb, it is no wonder that he felt that way.

And yet here we are, 101 years later. The American dream of a young,
Basque boy has inspired generations after him to love the sheep industry. Talbott Sheep Company and Star Creek Land Stewards are thriv-
ing, well-respected companies because of this. We keep our standards of
care and work high, just as Ramon taught our Aitachi Ray, and it shows
to those who come into contact with us. We deal with our challenges as

they come, and boy do they come. We adapt and we change, we continue to evolve, and we step up when necessary.

Importantly, throughout four generations, the women have stepped up. Marie Jeanne, Elena, and Teresa helped run their husbands' businesses, often without public acknowledgment or title. When the businesses were in need, they helped diversify and keep them afloat, and they're undoubtedly the reason we are still here today. It is no wonder that Andrée and Bianca continue the legacy of Talbott Sheep Co. When we think about it, it makes sense that our Aitachi has always emphasized the importance of Jose Artadi's question to Mrs. Talbott. Our family and Talbott Sheep Company exist today because Mrs. Talbott said, "Yes, we will have him."

Five Gold Coins and Seven Generations Later

DINA MOORE, TEAL CODY, AND LAUREN SIZEMORE

As the story goes, the Lone Star Ranch was purchased in January of 1896 by Thomas Hunter with five gold coins. It has been in the family since that time and has been passed down from Thomas to Frank Hunter, to Billy Hunter, to Ora Hunter Emerson, to Edra Emerson Moore, and to Mark Moore, Edra's son and the fifth generation from Frank. There is a saying that the current generation is holding the trust of the past for future generations. We members of the fifth and sixth generations, with our active involvement in the current ranching operation, now hold that trust for our descendants.

So many stories of hardship and triumph have been passed down along with the ranch, which lies primarily along the North Fork of Yager Creek, a tributary of the Van Duzen River located in Kneeland, California. Our knowledge starts with 1920s stories that Edra passed down. There were the devastating winters of the early '30s. Edra, who was born on February 23, 1921, shared stories of her childhood, the winter when they ran out of hay and cut fir boughs for the cows to eat and lost most of their livestock. They also cut madrone and tan oak. It was extremely cold, the Mad River froze, and the cattle were so weak that they couldn't get up.

After that the family turned to raising sheep until they could get back into the cattle business. A chore of Edra's was taking the sheep from their bedding grounds to the Iaqua Buttes so they could graze during the day. There is a picture of her when she was around seven or eight years old, holding a bobcat that she had shot by herself when taking the sheep to the buttes. As time went by and as Edra's grandchildren grew up, sheep became a distant memory for Edra, and she rarely spoke of raising sheep. She was a cattle rancher!

She was educated at a one-room schoolhouse, and she ran a trapline as she rode her horse to school. Pelts were a valuable commodity for a girl and a family who needed extra cash during the Depression. After finishing the eighth grade, Edra had to move to town for high school, like the generations that have followed her. Today, Edra's great-grandchildren attend Kneeland School, a two-room schoolhouse, and likely will also have to move to town for high school. And although it's ninety years later, great-grandson Ryden doesn't get to ride his horse or run a trapline on his way to school, but he can wear his cowboy hat, boots, and chaps and cut school to watch his cattle sell annually at the local sale barn.

Going to town and getting mail were big deals. Back then mail came three days a week—today it still does. But back then life stopped when the mail came, it was an event, and throughout her life, Edra would wait for and read the post on "mail days."

Edra shared stories of the trip to town taking two days and of what it was like traveling in the car with her grandfather, who always smoked a big cigar. Today it is no big deal to go to town, and we think nothing about going to town several days a week if necessary. Until she passed, though, Edra always needed to know all about town when you got home: where you went, who you saw, and what you observed in the neighborhood.

One of the most magical places on the ranch is Yager Creek. Nearly two and a half miles of it run through the ranch. Generations of the family know the creek intimately. In the early 1960s Ora Emerson was riding a horse and fell off and broke her back in the creek. We often wonder what that trip out of the creek must have been like for her, as the only access was on horseback to the county road some four miles up the hill. After that she used crutches and never complained.

One Christmas Eve after Ora passed, some neighbors stopped by the ranch to honor her memory with a handle of vodka. They would not leave until the vodka was gone. It was a bleary Christmas morning for some of the adults.

Now we think nothing of running down to the creek in our side-by-sides. Mark remembers camping on Yager as a child. They would ride the horses down to the creek and spend a week there. One night a bull fight broke out in camp, and his father, Charlie, threw him up a tree into safety. Those bulls made a mess of camp. Today we have a "glamping" spot on Yager, where we have "developed" the most beautiful place, quite a step up from the early days of camping with the bulls.

The ranch was logged in 1963 and 1964, as were many ranches on the North Coast. Timber was taxed on its standing value rather than on its yield. The log market was at a historical high, and the ranch was heavily logged. This was a boon for Edra, as her heart was in cattle: the more trees that were cut, and the more range that was opened, the more cattle a person could run.

The practices at that time were so different from what they are today. Yager Creek was pushed to the side, and dozers ran up and down the creek bed. Logs were decked in the creek beds because these were among the few flat places that were easy to skid to and easy to haul out of. All the timber was pulled down to the creek, with skid roads running up the adjacent streams that fed into Yager. It was estimated that at least thirty loads of logs a day were hauled out of Yager Creek. It took two summers to log the ranch.

Then the one-hundred-year flood of 1964 hit, a Pineapple Express. All the roads blew out, and Yager unraveled, as did many other creeks and streams on the North Coast. The only way in and out of Humboldt County was via the county road that ran through the ranch.

One young man was caught in the "back country" in the storm. He had promised his mother he would make it to town for Christmas. He had ridden his horse as far as he could, gotten a ride in a truck, and ended up at the ranch. He hadn't eaten for a couple days, and the family pulled together all the leftovers from Christmas dinner, shared a little whiskey, and sent the traveler on his way.

It has taken years for the creek and ecosystem to recover from the 1964 flood and from the associated impacts that were exacerbated by land-management practices that contributed to the degradation. At that time folks had no idea of the impacts that their management would cause. It was a common practice to build roads differently and to log differently.

Today we have a nonindustrial timber-management plan, a permit for logging in a sustainable manner with CAL FIRE. We implemented road upgrades on eighty thousand acres in the midportion of the Van Duzen River watershed with our neighbors, upgrading, mitigating, and storm-proofing roads for one-hundred-year storm events.

In 2018 we hired a consultant, Dr. Carson Jeffres of the UC Davis

Center for Watershed Sciences, to conduct an assessment of aquatic ecology and of the general ecosystem function on North Fork Yager Creek. His study found that the general aquatic ecology of the creek appeared to be in a relatively pristine state. "The presence of sensitive taxa in the Lone Star Ranch reach of the creek indicates that fine sediment impacts are minimal, water temperatures remain relatively cool during the summer months, and refuge is found during winter flooding events," he wrote. Sensitive species like the salmonfly stonefly, Pacific giant salamander, and foothill yellow-legged frog are found in the creek. We have been fortunate enough to observe salmon runs up Yager in the winter and to see thousands of yellow-legged frogs on the creek during the summer.

Our relationship with wildlife is a constant. Edra saw her first coyote when she was six or seven as she was coming back in a buggy from picking up the mail with her mother. At that time many ranchers raised sheep, and both coyotes and lions were hunted and poisoned extensively. Today, we have sightings of lions frequently and see coyotes all the time, hear them in the spring and summer, and have encounters with them as we ride. When protecting their dens, these coyotes can be a little intimidating. Being stalked by a coyote making its distinctive call is an eerie feeling.

At times in the past, the deer population was low, as all the homesteaders and ranchers ate deer, especially during the Depression when they could not afford to eat their own livestock. Today, many of our neighbors struggle with managing the growing elk herds. *Knock on wood*, for whatever reason, we have not had an influx of elk . . . yet. Elk impact the carrying capacity of cattle (how much grazing forage there is) and cause substantial infrastructure damage.

Our wild turkey population has also grown, and we have raptors of all varieties. One year when we were bringing calves up the hill to brand, we observed a pair of golden eagles hanging around. As we gathered, we started finding calves that had been preyed on by the eagles. They had the telltale signs of "eagle strike" on their backs and over their shoulder blades. It was a sad situation as we had to put down several calves and ended up doctoring eight or so.

This lifestyle requires resiliency. We bank on the resiliency of ourselves, Mother Nature, and our ecosystem. Part of our responsibility is to find better ways to enhance our stewardship of this amazing landscape, which we are holding in trust. We try to manage our cattle in a way that enhances the range and diversity of that landscape. We work with wild-life that are part of this community in a way that supports the fisheries, migratory birds, and endangered species. We work to enhance our timberlands and to protect our oak woodlands. We try new practices that challenge us. As a child, Mark had a healthy fear of wildfire and of what it could do. Now we are trying to conduct prescribed burns on our landscape as a management tool.

Life here always challenges our old beliefs. We want our children and grandchildren to be grounded by the ranch and to share this unique lifestyle. We worry, as the generations before us did, about the viability of ranching and about how they will be able to carry it forward.

The preceding generations took care of the landscape and ecosystem to the best of their ability. We hope that through our efforts, the next generation will continue to move conservation and economic sustainability forward. One quote from Edra embodies a philosophy that was ingrained in Mark and which he has ingrained in his children:

"I love this land dearly. And I have never wanted to live anywhere else. Having lived all over the United States, this is the only place I have ever really wanted to be, and it means a great deal to me. Taking care of it is always one of the things that has been very important to me. I was brought up to take care of it to the best of my knowledge from the generations before me. I certainly want to pass it on to my children and grandchildren. I think it is a wonderful way to live and a marvelous life."

Meadow Pasture

JESSICA SCHLEY

Earlier this year my father crossed through. I saw him go; on an old, red ranch horse of his, backdropped by a broad, white barn-back that blinds your eyes at sunrise despite its whitewash fading, like it does every sunny morning of every day of the year from dawn to noon.

His horse marched onward eagerly, though light blind, as was his confident custom in my father's gentle hands, working the cricket in his old Visalia bit, the one with no conchos or flare, just an old ranch bridle that worked and was well worn.

My daddy tipped his hat to avoid the sun blindness and just as trustingly put his faith in what neither the horse nor he could actually see ahead. It hardly mattered; they both knew the way and that the view from the ridge behind the barnyard corrals would be worth the squinting and the guessing as they made their way through the sunlight up the mare trail to the top of the hill.

He passed on through the hand-built, twenty-foot-tall, dirt-rust, redwood-plank, reinforced-steel gate frame at the back of the branding corral. The crossbar stood high enough above the gate that it was safe to ride through without ducking, but just like he always paused and bowed his head before sitting in a church pew, my father also always genuflected passing through that gate, hand on the latch as if on the crest of the pew.

From the branding corral through the old, slowly swinging, sturdy, iron gate—with rusty bolt hinges that sang in their grunting—came the view of the gentle middle pasture, the one our family saved for our mares in foal, the protected jewel at the center of the ranch, with the mellowest of swales and always thickest with shooting stars and chocolate lilies, a brook running through it, and plenty of oak nooks in the meadow for hiding foals in.

The gate closed behind him as he passed on out of the corrals with his sorrel horse, and afterward came that loud, reverberating, all-knowing, final clang. It's the kind of sound you know the meaning of when you hear it.

I saw him go. I watched it, and it was very slow. His horse's head, though carefully attentive, hung low. The cattle stopped grazing. A passing coyote pondered a far-off smell, head tipped in the direction that the old horseman was headed. The old, wide oak in the back corral was silent, but I could feel a warm breeze between her leaves and yet, in turn, a sad chill under the branches hanging closest to my cheeks.

An ancient oak within a square corral is a fitting enough foyer for me; and as that man I knew rode through those old gates and up that hill, backlit by the sunrise, I leaned into the shoulder of that rough-barked tree. For one brief moment, one second in eternal time, a kind, warm hand squeezed my shoulder, and I knew it was my father. And my dirt-coated, tear-stained cheek sank deeper into the gnarly thick bark of that tree.

Lord, Make Me an Oak Tree

Pamela Goforth Doiron

Lord, make me an oak tree.

Give me a strong taproot to keep me well grounded.

Give me a broad trunk to withstand fire and fury; a tough bark to repel hurts and abuse.

Make my branches strong enough to hold those who need me, but flexible enough to bend in the winds of change.

Let my limbs shelter those I love and my leaves provide a home to weaker souls.

Shower me with new green growth and purple buds as I reach to touch your face.

And in my old age, bring my ancient wooden body back to earth to warm and nourish those who will come after my time.

Fred Reyes

DICK GIBFORD

He grew up trottin' horseback
Behind his dad, Juan Reyes
A long-ridin' buckaroo
Who rode a center-fire kack
And threw a sixty-foot reata too.

Juan hired riders from here and Arizona
He ran a huge outfit just east
Of Cuyama Valley
Where they all rode together
The men of the "tie-hard"
And the men of the "dally."

Fred's dad and mom finally bought this ranch
The "Walking R"
It's all mountains
As rough as they come.

And here Juan raised Fred
To be all cowboy
As tough as they come.

Juan taught Fred to catch wild cattle
Rope them and tie 'em to a tree
Now Fred's cleaned out the wild ones
But still runs the tame ones
Into the 21st century.

I sure like ridin' for the "Walking R" Brand
And much like the wild cattle
Some of us cowboys have chose these mountains
To make our last stand.

The Cuyama

DICK GIBFORD

Red flint stone; serrated edge
By chalk-rock, sandstone outcropping
Hot desert wind whips through
Blue-green sage and on—
Into the sky
Shod hooves of caballo, cowboy,
Slide down the salt-brush-lined trail
To halt in the brown-brackish water
In the muddy bottom
Of the river, Cuyama.
The cattle tracks went downriver
Cowboy posts at a trot
Hot on the trail;
Other mounted cowboys converge
Bringing each his cattle to the trap.
The roundup done,
The cattle loaded,
Semitrucks are headed east
To Bakersfield.
The horses are unsaddled back at the ranch.
The cowboys head for the little desert town

To indulge in culinary
And adult beverage delights
At the Buckhorn.

Ah, the Buckhorn.
Inside the saloon
The north wall lined
With mounted heads of monster bucks
Donated by Lamar, Albert, and Emery Johnston,

And Emery's grandfather Gene,
One of the first Cuyama Forest Rangers
Appointed by Teddy Roosevelt.
He and J.D. Reyes
Now these men rode the country!
That was their job.
They were tough, reliable and resourceful.
Those were the times
When Gov't-appointed rangers
Spent 8–12 hours a day
In the saddle on patrol
From the Cuyama River to the Sisquoc.
"The Cuyama!"
A great place to spend a lifetime
—Or three.

To Whom It May Concern

GLORIA COTTRELL

Does it matter that there is more than one route to anywhere? It seems that a right-of-way agreement that has worked for forty years is still adequate for a new owner's use. Am I allowed to hold very dear the old homestead of Clarence and Jewel Pauline Schelling? This place where I can go to be alone and enjoy the quiet. A place where the sun for sure is shining brightly as the fog lays heavily on my house. This place that I put my heart into as I worked to keep that sweet, old house standing when others didn't understand why I liked it so much there.

The turtle lake that will actually show you a turtle, if you are patient. A lake that has wonderful water in winter and spring when we have enough rain and then reduces to pond lilies, cattails, and all sorts of strange vegetation as the weather warms. What a beautiful sight to see: a variety of wild ducks splashing about and showing off.

The mallard hen that flew across the lake yesterday thought I didn't know that she was taking my attention away from her ducklings. Always just beside the road in that little place where there is still enough water to show her ducklings how they can swim. Most likely a mallard hen that was hatched in the very same place. The lake where I took my grandson and showed him that I could call the ducks to him as he sat quietly waiting and was then disappointed that they were all hens and he wasn't allowed to shoot. Then there was the day that he bagged two drakes and had to take his shoes off and wade in to retrieve them. "Nana, we sure need a bird dog."

There is usually a flock of wild turkeys strutting around and a few buck deer grazing nearby. On a very warm day you can see the antlers of the bucks, who are lying in the nearly dry pond to cool off.

No traffic going by there, just peace and quiet. A place where five members of the Schelling family brought their father's ashes to spread in the area of the old millsite below the house just two years ago. They were so appreciative.

I will never forget all the ground-squirrel shooting I took Clayton there for. I think he got all of them. It was the best of times. Memories so valuable to me now that he has grown into a wonderful young man. I still love to go there to enjoy the quiet and the absence of traffic. Recently a bear left a paw print on the kitchen door. I still have not washed it off.

What was he thinking as he looked through the window? Maybe I'm glad I wasn't there that day.

The gate will remain locked as far as I'm concerned. Some things are just too precious to allow change. What is the value of peace of mind?

Postscript

After a long and costly process, the new landowner agreed to use and abide by the rules of the original right-of-way agreement through my ranch.

Saving the Sheep in the Snow

Marilyn Sagehorn Russell

Growing up on our beautiful 5,200-acre ranch in Mendocino County, California, has provided me many stories to tell, but my favorite involves rescuing our herd of sheep during an unusually snowy winter.

I had been on the ranch from age five (in the fall of 1948) until I enrolled at UC Berkeley in the fall of 1961, and to be truthful, I was seriously homesick for many months when I got to college. I couldn't wait for the holidays and the long summer vacation so I could return to the ranch and resume outside work on the range. In January of 1963 there was a heavy snowstorm in Mendocino County; the snow built up to over four feet in the higher elevations and, with a cold front, stayed on the ground for more than two weeks. Unfortunately, my dad came down with a gallbladder infection and was bedridden this entire time. We had about eight hundred ewes ready to lamb that he had not been able to gather to the big barn at the homeplace. Back in Berkeley, I was frantic and was able to convince my professors to allow me to take my finals early so that I could head for home. The local game warden met me at the Greyhound bus station in Willits, and with four-wheel drive, he was able to get me home.

The next morning, I saddled up our big buckskin gelding, Buck, took my dad's best shepherd dog, Lad, and headed toward the most northern pasture. The upper portions of our ranch are divided into four big pastures, approximately one thousand acres each. All the gates were open, so we didn't know where the sheep were. I rode for three days, checking methodically from north to south. The sun was bright, but the snow was crystalized and did not melt. I used charcoal from the burned trees (from a big fire in 1950—another story) to help shield my eyes from the blinding snow. We didn't seem to have dark glasses in those days!

I became more discouraged with each passing day, and as I prepared for the fourth day and a search of the last section, my dad told me that if there were any lambs, I should just kill them and get the ewes home.

Miracle of miracles, I found most of the herd in a canyon about two miles from the open county road leading to the homeplace. They were in a long line, facing away from home and stuck in the snow. I was able to start at one end and turn each sheep around. Then began the slow, laborious process of breaking trail toward home. I would lead the horse behind me, clear out a few hundred feet, and then get the sheep going along this alleyway of snow until they reached the end of the cleared pathway; then I would have to go back to the front of the herd and step out another clearing. I know I started early in the morning and didn't reach the county road until about two o'clock.

About the lambs . . . there were five, and I couldn't kill or leave them. So, I tied their legs together and hung them over the saddle horn of that good ranch horse! One ewe was too weak to move, and I left her. I can still see her looking at me as we moved away. But I'm thankful there was only one in this condition out of the entire herd.

We moved along slowly and methodically for several hours, and the dog helped keep the line going through the snow, which eventually petered out as we neared the main county road. Happily, another miracle occurred! My dad, mom, and brother (who had developmental challenges and could not do this kind of riding) were there with the Jeep and a load of alfalfa hay, which they used to entice the ewes to the safety of the barn a mile and a half away. I just kept them going from the rear, and we made it back safely just as it got dark. It was such a good feeling to have those ewes in the barn. I can still hear them munching on hay, one of the best sounds I could imagine! And those five lambs made it just fine too. We got them connected to their moms, who were happy to nurse them from full udders.

We ran both sheep and cattle, but I think it was the combination of wool and lambs that provided the finances to put me through UC Berkeley. I am honored that I could help save our herd during that cold winter. To this day, I love remembering that entire adventure even though the days were long and cold. Our ranch was and is a beautiful landscape. (Snow is fairly rare in our area of California, so I really enjoy it!) I appreciate the fact that I could ride alone for several days with a serious responsibility to assist my family and to protect the income for the ranch. I still love to ride and work livestock. I truly appreciate the resilience that my childhood forged in me!

Small-Town Girl Goes Ranching

PENNY SAMPERT SCRIBNER

The phone rang on a Friday night in the fall of 1958, not long after my junior year of high school had started. I thought it would be my boy-friend, Johnny. Instead, it was his older brother, Bob. "Need your help," he said. It seemed that Clayton Charlie, a fellow rancher, had a cow that broke from the herd as he was bringing the bunch down from the high country to winter pasture. Clayton suspected that her calf, born in late summer, had tired and wandered off to lie down. Back at the home ranch, when the ear tag numbers were checked, hers was missing. Each fall at the end of the open range season, the Forest Service locked the gates to the high country. This cow and calf were behind the locked gates. Clay-ton had his hands full so called Bob to ask if he could help.

I jumped at the prospect of riding with Bob to look for the pair; I never gave up the chance to work cattle. I cleared it with my parents and went to bed with the intent of rising early.

Bob's wife, Tessie Ragsdale Fisher, was my 4-H horse project leader. She and Bob lived on Biddle Road near the Medford airport, about five miles from my house, which was near Jacksonville, Oregon. They were soon to move to the Ragsdale family ranch at Lake Creek. Tessie was pregnant at the time and unable to ride. I was the backup wrangler.

That morning, I saddled Misty in the dark and rode the miles across town, arriving at the Fishers' house in time for hot, black coffee (lots of sugar available), eggs, bacon, and piles of toast. Parked out front was the one-ton Chevy with a stock rack that could handle three or four saddled horses. After breakfast we bundled up, dropped the ramp, and loaded up Bob's horse— Nipper—and Misty. Not far out of town, we pulled off Crater Lake Highway near Eagle Point to pick up two more horses and riders, Larry Perry and Sharon Forde, another 4-H-er. We then turned south, hitting a logging road that headed toward Howard Lake. As we climbed into the Cascades, snow began to swirl in the headlights, slowing us to a crawl. The truck didn't have a heater, but it didn't matter much with the four of us crammed in the front seat.

Larry Perry worked for some government office, so he had a key to unlock the Forest Service padlock. On our side of the gate were corrals and a loading chute. We left the gate to the corrals open and swung the Forest Service metal-pipe gate away from the road and into the ditch. If we found the pair, we hoped to haze them in.

We rode out into the woods with a headwind blowing fine, pelting snow, and we called, "Soou-ee . . . soou-eee," as we went. We split into two groups, agreeing to be back at the truck by noon whether we found the pair or not. Bob and I pulled our wool hats down and hunkered over the pommels of our saddles. I had forgotten my gloves, so I put one hand under my thigh and the other on the reins, switching back and forth. We figured that we'd find a dead calf and maybe a crazed cow.

About an hour out, Misty threw up her head and perked up her ears. Looking through the underbrush and firs, we saw two red and white ears. This was not a buck. This was a cow. She snorted, then crashed, spun, stopped, and stared back. She knew horses. Whatever goes through a cow's brain we'll never know, but at some level she knew that seeing a horse and rider was her ticket out of the forest. The calf was with her, a sturdy bull calf. Mama didn't look too much worse for wear, a little thin as ice and snow had covered what remaining grass there was. Bob and I gave her some room to settle, and then we eased Misty and Nipper around to head her back. As we approached the corrals, Larry and Sharon rode out from our right. When they saw the cow and calf, they dropped behind. Down the frozen, rutted road we went toward the gate. In the bitter cold, Bob pulled out a flask of whisky, handing it to me. It burned my throat as it gave heat and fire. I reached over to Sharon. She grumbled about how cold she was and refused the flask, making herself even more miserable. I thought to myself, *She's more trouble than the cow and calf.*

As we neared the pipe gate and the corrals, we fanned out to the sides, not wanting the cow to bolt. We eased the pair into the corral, closed the gate, tossed in a half bale of hay, and loaded up the horses. Clayton would pick them up the next day. Job well done.

Lake Creek Ranch

Summary of 1959

PENNY SAMPERT SCRIBNER

By the summer of 1959, Bob and Tessie had moved to the home ranch near Lake Creek. Tessie's folks, Dorothea and Wallace (known as Ganki) Ragsdale, lived in the main house, a one-story ranch. Bob and Tessie, having moved from Biddle Road, took up residence in the original, square farmhouse, a two-story, white clapboard on the knoll near the barn. Known as the Big House, it had running water in the kitchen, a claw foot bathtub on the back porch, and a privy in the backyard. A woodstove heated the front room in the winter, and a wood cookstove with an incinerator warmed the kitchen.

That summer found me looking for work. I was sixteen at the time and had recently returned home from Oregon State's summer school program for 4-H Junior Leaders. I landed a job flipping hamburgers and making milkshakes at the Medford Airport Café. The first day on the job was also my last. The milkshake machine and I had a disagreement. The next day I was up early, saddling my horse, Misty, to ride to the Wine Glass Three Ranch at Lake Creek, located about twenty miles out of Medford. Bob and Tessie offered me a job driving tractor in the hayfields.

My bedroom, up the steep stairs, was over the kitchen. Johnny, my boyfriend and Bob's younger brother, slept out on the porch. Marvin Terry, a couple years older, drove to the ranch each morning. We were up and moving while the stars were still out. Tessie would make us a ranch breakfast of eggs, fried potatoes, and toast slathered with churned butter courtesy of Daisy, the milk cow.

The herd of about two hundred cows and calves had been moved up country to the open range for the summer, leaving the home meadows to grow oat, timothy, and rye grasses for the hay. By the time I arrived, the hay in both the Upper Meadow and the Lower Meadow lay in wind-rows. Bob ran the baler. The grass hay was baled into two-string bales weighing about thirty-five to forty pounds each. After a quick lesson, I drove tractor with Johnny on one side and Marv on the other, each buck-ing the bales onto the flatbed of the trailer. The Lower Meadow's load was maneuvered across a creek and uneven ground to the large livestock barn in the lot just down from the Big House. Once there, Johnny and Marv would use a pulley to hoist the bales up into the hayloft. In the Upper Meadow, we piled the hay into an open-air stack, which grew and which we later covered with black, plastic tarps. The cows would spend much of the winter there.

While I was out in the hay field, Tessie and Dorothea were hard at work in the kitchen at the main house. By lunchtime the hay crew had been out in the fields for six to seven hours. We would come in from the field, wash up using the hose and basin by the back door, then shuffle in to sit at a table groaning with fried chicken or roasted ranch beef, gravy, potatoes, biscuits, garden beans, tomatoes, and always some sort of pie. After lunch we'd often sprawl out on the cool grass next to the house under a large oak. Later, toward evening as it cooled off, we'd head out for one last load before calling it quits. Then it was time to get out the church key and have a cold Olympia.

One particular day stands out in my memory. Just before noon, we were finishing up the last load from the Lower Meadow. As I inched the tractor along to the creek, I felt the load begin to shift. In an effort to keep it upright, I tried to back up to come at the creek from a slightly differ-ent angle. The trailer jackknifed, hit the creekbank, and tipped over the entire load. One trailer tire spun in the air. At first Johnny and Marv were angry and let out a yell as they jumped off the stack; then they thought it was hilarious that I didn't know how to back up a trailer. We were late for lunch that day.

The razzing continued right up to dessert as Dorothea proudly put that day's pie down in front of Ganki, announcing that this was his favor-ite: mincemeat. It was the end of haying season, which was cause for cel-ebration. The pie did look delicious. My mom made mincemeat pie for the holidays. It was one of my favorites too. I looked around, and no one else seemed to be helping themselves except Ganki. Ignoring the two boys, I took the big piece offered to me and dove right in. What was it? It sure wasn't like my mom's. The boys knew and watched me take that first bite. My eyes watered and I couldn't seem to chew, fighting off the urge to gag. Johnny sputtered, "Bear meat!" Sure enough, it was homemade bear mincemeat, stringy and tough. I carefully took my napkin, wiped my mouth, pretending to chew. Gales of laughter followed me as I left the table, napkin in hand.

On August 2 I saddled Misty to ride home: my summer job was over. As we were leaving, Bob waved me down, saying he might need a hand bringing the cows home from the summer range. He'd give me a call. Tessie was again pregnant that summer. She had miscarried once before and was having a difficult time.

Late August came, the Jackson County Fair was over, and school would be starting the next week. Bob did call and asked if I could come for the week. Bored at home, I was eager to go. Back up at the ranch, Misty and I fell into our routine. During haying season, it had been our job to bring Daisy up from the Lower Meadow each evening for milking. Daisy would often hide out at the far end of the field. Now that the hay was off the field, the ditches were open, letting the irrigation water flood the field. Misty and I would gallop across, jumping ditches and spraying water as we went. I would let out a whoop and a holler, and Misty, ears pricked, would let out a kick.

That weekend Bob saddled up Grey, a large, heavy-boned gelding capable of working a long day. I packed our lunches into my saddle-bag and saddled Misty. We rode out together as the sun rose. The ranch backed up to the shoulders of the Southern Cascades. We jogged the dirt road to the Tice Place, past their barn and outbuildings, leaving the last of any dwellings behind. When we got there, Bob opened the gate to the High Cascades Ranger District-Butte Falls. We rode though towering ponderosas, dodging scattered scrub oaks and an occasional cedar. At the first clearing Bob said, "I'm headed out that way." He flung his left arm out to the west. "I want you to ride up on that ridge." He pointed north. "Then," he said, "you'll hit a fence. Turn west," he nodded left, "ride that fence line to the corner, and open the gate. Wait for me there. And don't get in the way." Before I could respond, he turned and put Grey into a high trot.

I sat on Misty and looked up toward the ridge. I had just a moment of panic before I turned her uphill. We wove our way through the scattered lava rocks, outcroppings, and buckbrush and occasionally criss-crossed streams. The ridge seemed elusive and didn't seem to be getting any closer. Blue jays chattered, and Misty's shoes clattered against an occasional rock. The smell of dry grass and pine needles warmed by the sun settled my nerves. This was all new country for me, and I was truly alone. I remembered what my forester dad had told me: "Always follow water downhill." I looked at the creeks and thought, *I bet they empty into Little Butte Creek near the ranch. I could find my way back, if need be.* That was a comfort. Misty seemed confident and strong as she climbed. Out of seemingly nowhere, a three-strand, barbed-wire fence appeared. I turned Misty to the left and looked back over the valley below. *How much time has gone by; an hour, two?* I looked at the sun. It wasn't yet noon. *How far is the gate?* I wondered.

Following the fence line, weaving in and out of the timber, we continued, as another hour passed. At the far end of an open meadow, I saw a cross fence dipping over the downhill edge. *That must be the corner,* I realized, and sighed with relief. At the gate, I dismounted, letting Misty grab a mouthful of grass. I faced a portagee gate: a section of four strands of barbed-wire fencing held to the gatepost by a loop of wire at the top and bottom. It was strung tight. In order to release it, I needed to take the baseball-bat-sized stick that hung from a rawhide rope and try to pry the gate toward the post to ease the tension and let it open. No luck. I tried again. I just wasn't strong enough. Meanwhile Misty had moved away and was working her way along the edge of the meadow. I dropped the stick and eased toward her, saying, "Whoa, whoa, whoa," snapped the halter rope to the ring, and tied her up high on a sapling. Back to the gate. My heart was pounding as I realized that Misty could have easily headed for home. *What was I thinking?* I realized I needed to not only make it my habit to ride with a halter under the bridle, one with a rope tied in a bowline around Misty's neck, but also *to use* that rope to tie her up.

What was I hearing? "Soou-ee . . . soou-eee." The cows! Bob was calling the cows. My adrenaline kicked in, and with one more herculean effort, I pried the gate open and flung it back on itself. Now, how to stay out of the way, so as not to frighten and scatter the cows? I quickly untied Misty and moved her down the fence line out of sight. The cows flowed through the gate, followed by Bob.

Later that evening, down by the barn, after we had mothered up cows and calves and counted the pairs, Bob turned to me. "Good job, cowgirl." He smiled.

Upper Meadow

Winter of 1959–60

Penny Sampert Scribner

While I was driving tractor, riding Misty to and from the Wine Glass Three Ranch, bringing in Daisy at milking time, and moving cows from the high country, my parents were going through the struggle of their lives. There was a shake-up at the Elk Lumber Company, where my dad was production manager, and he resigned. Beginning in February he would be teaching forestry at the University of California, Berkeley. My parents immediately put our home on Renault Avenue up for sale and began to pack. It was a tumultuous time for our family.

It was my senior year at Medford High. What would they do with me? And the animals? I had two horses, Misty and my stud colt, Ras-Rif (Razy), two 4-H steers, our dog, Kelly, and our cat, Freckles. Decisions were made. Kelly would find a new home on a turkey ranch outside of town. Freckles would move to Berkeley. Those were the easy decisions. Time was running out as we cut and trimmed our last silvertip Christmas tree. To this day I am not sure how those final decisions and arrangements were made. As it turned out, I was to move to Lake Creek along with the horses and two steers to live with Bob and Tessie. Young people themselves, Tessie, age twenty-two, and Bob, age twenty-four, agreed to take in sixteen-year-old me so I could finish out the year. I agreed to be kitchen help and a ranch hand in return for my room and board.

Sometime between Christmas and New Year's 1960, my parents put all their worldly goods in storage and left for California. They left Mom's 1949 Studebaker for me to drive the twenty-some miles from Lake Creek to Medford High. Bob helped me move the two steers to a shed behind the Big House. I was to have the same bedroom, upstairs over the kitchen, that I had had during the summer.

Because it was winter and I was in school, Bob moved Misty up in the cattle truck. But there was a glitch. A serious glitch. Razy, my three-year-old Arab colt, had strangles, a sometimes-fatal respiratory disease that results in abscesses in the lymph tissue under a horse's jaw, at the throat-latch. It is quite contagious. Where he had picked it up, we didn't know. What we did know is that he couldn't be around other horses. And in fact, he could barely move. Razy was down in his stall, next to our recently sold house. He needed to stand. My 4-H records from those days show that the vet, Doc Phillips, came every afternoon after school from January 4 through January 18. He would help get Razy on his feet, lance and drain the boils, and medicate him. As Razy improved, Doc Phillips taught me how to drain the boils and apply hot compresses. This meant I left school, drove back to Renault Avenue, met the vet, cared for Razy, mucked out his stall, then drove to Lake Creek to feed steers, help Tessie, and do my homework. At sixteen I had plenty of energy and could do the work of it.

The difficulty was that the people who had bought our house were hostile toward me. It was a typical Rogue River valley winter, cold, wet, and foggy. I struggled to change from my school shoes into boots and a work jacket to deal with Razy. I found myself pretty much living out of the trunk of the Studebaker. The buyers finally agreed to let me put my galoshes on inside the back door of the garage and plug in a hot plate to make hot water for the compresses. That helped. My 4-H records also show that Razy finally moved to the ranch on February 22. Soon after, I was riding him to the Upper Meadow when I went to feed the cows each morning.

The end of February and early March found me using the privy out back while checking out the stars, making coffee, and heading for the barn with Bob. Tessie was pregnant again and this time more determined than ever to hold on to her pregnancy. Bob and I would saddle up and then ride the muddy, rock-strewn trail to the Upper Meadow. There, we'd fire up the Allis Chalmer tractor. I'd drive "Alice" through the herd of two hundred pregnant and calving cows while Bob popped the strings from the bales. We'd count the new calves, making notes for Tessie; she kept meticulous ranch records. One day melded into another.

One winter morning stands out in my memory. There was frost on the path to the privy, and brilliant stars dotted the black sky. Soon after closing the privy door, I heard the growl of a bear. Now what? Realizing I couldn't stay in there forever, I decided to make a mad dash for it. The "bear" was Bob. He burst into laughter!

The morning ride to the Upper Meadow became routine and some-times even magical. While the cows munched, we loaded the trailer for the next morning's feeding. At the beginning of February, the stack loomed over my head. By the time the last calf was born in early March, it had dwindled to a few broken bales. It was time to move the herd down to the barn lot.

The second week of March was spring vacation. It was branding time. A spring ritual: One needed to mark the young stock before set-ting them loose to grow up in the high country over the coming summer. The Wine Glass Three brand reached all the way back to the original one hundred Oregon brands set down in longhand by the area's first ranchers. It was Tessie's great-grandfather's brand. I spent the week helping with the branding, with ear tagging and castrating the bull calves, with moth-ering up and counting each pair. Other ranchers came to help. Bawling cows, crying calves, smoke, laughter, and the smell of burnt flesh and frying mountain oysters filled the air. Tessie, pregnant with her daugh-ter-to-be, sat on the corral rails writing down the number of each cow's ear tag and whether each calf was a bull (now a steer) or a heifer, as she eyed them one by one. She also made notes about their condition. Would this heifer be a good replacement for that old cow?

At the end of the week, we turned the herd out into the alfalfa field next to the Big House, giving them a week to settle. It would then be time to move the herd up country to summer pasture. I could imagine another summer of driving tractor, building a new stack of hay in the Upper Meadow, and riding up country to salt the cows. But that is not what hap-pened. This small-town girl was about to head to Berkeley.

McBride Livestock Ranches

Walt Giacomini

My freshman year at Cal Poly, I lived in the dorms. At the start of my sophomore year, I moved off campus into a small, ancient, adobe house in an older part of town. My roommates were John Ford and Andy McBride. John and I had known each other our entire lives, but I had never met Andy.

He was several years older than I was, but we were on track to graduate at the same time. By the end of our senior year, we were good friends. I knew that I wanted to learn the ranching business and that I wanted to live in Humboldt County, so it was a natural fit for me to go to work for McBride Livestock Ranches, owned by Andy's mother. Viola McBride was the granddaughter of Joseph Russ, who had come to California during the Gold Rush. What made things interesting was that I was coming on board as the green ranch hand; Andy was coming home to be the manager.

The ranching operation was a large, diversified outfit with headquarters located near where Salmon Creek drains into Humboldt Bay (now a U.S. Fish and Wildlife Service refuge). In addition to pasture, the Salmon Creek Ranch produced barley, hay, and silage. Most of the cattle and sheep were run on the McBrides' Bear River ranches, Southmayd, Bonanza, Seattle, The Johnston, Central Park, Spicy Breezes, and Dublin Heights.

To work for McBride Livestock Ranches in the mid-sixties was to be a part of Humboldt County ranching that was about to fade into history. It was one of the last big outfits to maintain a bunkhouse and a cookhouse. The people who worked there were unique, not only in who they were but also because the jobs they held were about to change or to be eliminated.

Jimmy Collins was the foreman. He was not the kind of boss who told people what to do. He just went to work, and if you were working with him, you were expected to keep up. Jimmy worked hard, and he chewed on his cigar just as hard. It always went out shortly after being lit. It still got used up, however; instead of disappearing as it burnt, it went away from the other end. After an hour or so, no more cigar.

In the late sixties, he celebrated fifty years of employment and his "retirement," but he just kept working. When he could no longer work all day, every day, he continued to show up to do what he could, and Viola McBride kept paying him as if he were still the foreman. By the early nineties, I had taken over the operation of much of the McBride properties, and he still showed up occasionally to help, and Viola continued to pay him.

While Jimmy did most of his work at Salmon Creek, Charlie Larsen was in charge of the Bear River Ranches and the Salmon Creek livestock. Other than a stint in the U.S. Cavalry during the thirties, he had spent most of his adult life working for various descendants of Joseph Russ.

Charlie was an excellent stockman, proficient at managing both sheep and cattle. He was also a bit of a curmudgeon. I was green as grass, but he tolerated me reasonably well most of the time. I strained our relationship, however, when one day at lunchtime, I put the mare I had been riding into a small pen with his gelding. My horse kicked his, putting the gelding out of commission for some time. It took Charlie a while to get over that. He did advise me as I acquired a decent saddle and other tack, and when he learned that I was a college-educated horse breaker, he arranged for me to start a filly owned by Joe Russ III, Viola's first cousin.

Another ranch hand, Louie Ballister, had left the Coast Guard a year or so before coming to work with Charlie. Louie was good with stock but had the "disadvantage" of also being very capable with machinery. With its extensive grain, hay, and silage enterprises, the McBride outfit used a lot of machinery in the sixties.

It became apparent that when Andy arranged for me to be hired, he planned on taking greater advantage of Louie's equipment skills by having him spend more time at Salmon Creek and having me spend most of my time helping Charlie at Bear River. Louie was a good soldier, and while reluctant, he may have been willing to take one for the team, but Charlie didn't like this new plan at all.

When more than two people were needed for livestock work, I did get to be part of the crew. On one of our rides to Bear River, I told Louie and Charlie that at some point, I intended to be a rancher. To say that they failed to take me seriously would be an understatement.

When less than three men were needed for livestock work, I was stuck at Salmon Creek, doing work that I hadn't signed on for. Charlie came up with a solution. He consulted with Andy, then talked to Joe Russ, and the end result was that I went to work for Joe after spending just a summer with McBrides.

The time I spent working with Charlie and Louie really helped me to begin to acquire the skills needed to become a competent hand. Charlie was a good, if not always patient, teacher, and Louie was particularly helpful to me. In addition, in spite of the failure to create an entry-level cowboy job for me, Andy continued to be my good friend. Our relationship only strengthened over the years and contributed to some huge changes in the lives of the Giacominis and the McBrides later on.

Bill, Pete, and the Way It Was

Walt Giacomini

In late August 1964 I went to work for Joe Russ at the Ocean House, at Cape Mendocino. The outfit was just beginning to wean calves, so I anticipated plenty of cowboy work right away. The boss had a different plan for me. As Joe, his sons Jack and Joe IV, and Rich Holland saddled up, loaded up, and headed to Forest Home Ranch, I was sent several miles down the road toward Petrolia to repair fence. I was very disappointed. This was a common practice, to test the new kid to see if he was willing to do the less interesting work. To be a cowboy, you had to be willing to do non-cowboy work. Apparently, I passed the test, and was included on the weaning crew for the rest of the fall.

In October I was sent to live and work at the Ocean Ranch, just south of the Table Bluff Lighthouse near Loleta, California. This ranch was leased from the Murphy family, who also owned the Pacific Lumber Company. I spent the rest of the fall helping with weaning, caring for weaned calves at the Ocean Ranch, and, with Rich Holland, building a set of corrals at the Valley View Ranch, one of three other ranches owned or leased by the Russ family along Copenhagen Road, southeast of the Ocean Ranch.

Living by myself was a lonesome affair. The house, situated on high ground, was a huge, old, two-story place that may have been considered a mansion in its day. When I moved in, luxurious it was not. The roof leaked, it was damp and drafty, and the only heat was provided by a fireplace. I figured out that the only way to be comfortable in the morning was to lay a fire in the fireplace before I crawled into my bedroll, which I placed on a cot, within reach of the fireplace. I would light the fire in the morning before getting out of bed.

Bill Counts, a gregarious old gentleman, lived in a small house nearby. If Bill was to be believed, he had enjoyed a more exciting and interesting life than all of the Texas Rangers, the Earp brothers, and Don Juan combined. He loved to tell of his adventures, and after a time his stories began to register as familiar. They sounded like stories I had read in pulp western magazines. Whether Bill had lived or read about these adventures, at this point in his life he was sure that he had been there. At any rate, listening to his tales provided great entertainment.

Bill was well into his eighties and unable to do much anymore. Until I moved onto the place, he had served as a caretaker. It was the end of an era for his kind. In the mid-sixties nearly every ranch of any size had a guy like Bill on the place.

Most were single. Some were young enough to take care of day-to-day ranch work. Some just kept the water running and patched a little fence. Others were able to cook when the crew came around to do the big jobs. Some, like Bill, could do little more than call the boss if something appeared to be amiss.

Many of these men had a problem with alcohol. Most understood and respected the rule that no alcohol was permitted on the premises. They would abstain while at the ranch, then go to town for a weekend, once a month or so. Those weekends often stretched out to as much as a week. By the fourth day, the boss was ready to fire them, but by the sixth or seventh day, if they were otherwise good employees, reason prevailed, and the boss was glad to get them back.

My favorite among these guys was Pete Pedrotti. A shirttail relative of mine, Pete's abilities were limited. He had Down syndrome characteristics but did seem to function at a higher level than most people with those challenges. He could drive a jeep or a tractor (if the terrain wasn't too challenging), feed the dogs and horses, and fix fence. He also served as my cook when I was at the Ocean House ranch headquarters, when Joe and Annetta weren't there.

The first time he cooked for me, he prepared a combination of macaroni and some kind of meat. I knew that one should stay on the good side of the cook, so I went overboard with praise for his concoction. Big mistake. From then on, it was macaroni and mystery meat, every night.

Pete loved to build model wagons and stagecoaches. I told him that I sure would like him to build one for me. His raw materials were wood from old fruit boxes and anything else that was handy. He had a small electric jigsaw, as well as some crude hand tools. His physical challenges made him quite clumsy. His fingers and hands were huge and not nimble. He built me a chuck wagon, complete with tarp, drop-down tailgate, pots, pans, coffeepot, water barrel with a working valve, working brakes, and harness for the model horses he purchased. All the wheels turned. The steering, suspension, and harness were exact replicas of the real thing. It took him twenty tries to cut out and assemble the four wheels. I've had the wagon for over fifty years, and it has always been prominently displayed, wherever I have lived.

Brands and Branding

WALT GIACOMINI

Hot-iron branding is a useful tool for identifying livestock. As technology has progressed, alternative identification methods have developed, but none combine the critical characteristics of permanence and of visibility at a distance that the hot-iron brand provides. Evidence exists that branding was used by ancient Egyptians nearly five thousand years ago. Its usefulness has truly stood the test of time.

As the general population has gotten farther away from our agricultural roots, individuals and groups have increasingly exerted pressure on ranchers to stop branding. There is some pain as the brand is applied, but it is very short-lived. Once the heat affects the nerve endings on the surface of the hide, the pain goes away. A calf will squirm at first but will relax within seconds.

The first pioneers, as they settled in the American West, had little need for a brand. Their neighbors were few and far away. As the ranching population grew, and the need for effective identification increased, branding became more widespread. Branded cattle were more likely to be returned by honest neighbors and less likely to be stolen by the dishonest. The trail drives from Texas to northern shipping points, where thousands of cattle were driven hundreds of miles, increased the need to prove ownership. Herds could get mixed up on the trail or mixed in with cattle in the country being driven through. As cattle herds expanded on the unfenced western prairie, filling the void created by the eradication of the bison, they grazed in common. Herds were only handled twice a year, at branding and at shipping. This required cooperation, and shared labor, between owners of the cattle, and a way to easily identify who owned which cattle.

When I went to work at the Ocean House for Joe Russ III in 1964, he used what he called the double U brand, not to be confused with, as he put it, the "double ya." The double U was two connected U's, as opposed to a W, which brings up the point: a brand needs to be expressible in words, not some exotic, indescribable figure.

In the 1960s nearly every calf branded in Humboldt County was run through a calf chute, a smaller version of the mechanical device used to restrain cows and bulls. Things began to change in the seventies. By then I had returned to the McBride Livestock Ranches owned by Viola McBride. One of my jobs was calving the first-calf heifers. Louie Ballister was the foreman then, and he, Al Cooper, Dan Domenighini, and I, along with a ground crew, roped and branded the heifer's calves instead of using the chute. I know that John Rice and Martin Gift began to help each other rope and brand some of their calves in the late seventies. Later, Bill McBride, Andy's brother, and Andy's foreman, Lou Bugenig, began to rope both Andy's and Bill's calves. I would estimate that the majority of the calves in Humboldt County are now roped when branded.

Some may think that replacing a calf chute with a rope is reversing progress. Old skills and traditions have value, however. Done right, roping when branding takes advantage of and enhances the skills of both horse and horseman. Also, if done right, it is less stressful on the calf as it avoids the collision of calf and steel that occurs when using a chute. Calves that are roped, instead of running through a chute, seem to have more respect for a horse, which makes handling them easier as they get older. There are benefits outside the branding pen as well. Northern California terrain is steep and rough, and it is often impractical, even impossible, to get a cow that needs treatment to a corral. It is very difficult to rope outside on an inexperienced horse; dangerous if you manage the catch.

When branding, ropers and ground crew should work together to catch, restrain, and work calves with minimal stress on calf, horse, and crew. Competition is fine in a contest, but not when you have several ropers and maybe twice as many helpers on the ground. A big wreck may seem entertaining, after the fact, if no one is seriously injured, but I want no part of one at my branding.

It takes four or five people to brand a large number of calves using a chute. It takes at least twice that many when roping. Few California ranches employ crews of that size. That means that friends and neighbors have to help each other. We get a chance to visit, enjoy the spring weather, and turn a hard, physical job into enjoyable work. It's as close to an old-fashioned barn raising as we are likely to experience in this day and age. We also have the opportunity to learn how other people do things. I have never visited someone else's ranch without learning something new. Sometimes you learn what not to do; but that's okay too.

Last Cattle Drive

In 1980 Andy McBride's operation included ranches at Salmon Creek, Centerville, and Bear River, from West Point to Dublin Heights. Lou Bugenig was the overall foreman for the ranches, and I worked under him as the foreman at Salmon Creek. We had heard all the historical stories about livestock (turkeys, even) that had been driven overland and down the beach from Petrolia to Fernbridge. And now, in the fall of 1980, we needed to move 163 coming three-year-old, first-calf heifers from Fern Cottage to Bear River.

Because Andy's operations bordered the ocean at both Fern Cottage and in the hills, it made sense for us to try to recreate what had been done in the past. After consulting a tide book, scouting the beach, and planning a route from Fern Cottage—down the beach to Oil Creek, up through West Point, across Mazeppa, Central Park, and the Peters Place, and up a newly constructed road on the north side of Spicy Breezes— we determined that the drive was doable. We planned a three-day trip, beginning on September 24, with stops at West Point and Central Park before ending in the Mailbox Pasture at Spicy Breezes.

It was originally decided that Andy, his brother Bill, Lou Bugenig, Francie Bugenig, Charlie Hower, Bill Clow, and I would make the drive. As word spread, however, the size of the crew doubled. Lots of folks wanted to be part of revisiting the way things used to be. We had to plan our departure time from the Fern Cottage corrals so that we would pass the area between Guthrie Creek and Oil Creek at low tide. Under normal conditions, working or driving cattle during the middle of the day on the North Coast is not a problem; but, as it turned out, this day— which had a high of at least 80 degrees—was one of the hottest September days on record. To add to the challenge, the heifers were very fat, having spent the summer on the lush valley feed.

We headed west from the corrals. We ran into trouble as soon as we hit the dunes between the pasture and the ocean. With some difficulty, we got the herd bunched up and headed south.

Our intent was to keep the cattle moving on the wave slope, where we assumed the going would be easier on the wet, packed sand. The sand was wet. Unfortunately, it was also very coarse, so it was loose as well. This made the going hard for the cattle, although it did serve to settle them down, at least at the start.

As we approached Centerville, we were amazed to see that a crowd had gathered. Dozens of people, plus all the local TV stations, were on hand. We got pretty puffed up at the idea of being central characters in such a colorful, historical recreation. Well, as the saying goes, pride goeth before a fall.

As we arrived at Fleener Creek, we decided to hold the cattle up and allow them to rest from slogging through the deep sand. We needed about an hour, anyway, for the timing to be right to get around the bluffs between Guthrie Creek and Oil Creek at low tide. After resting, the cattle were rarin' to go, and we headed on down the beach.

In preparation for the drive, Andy had built a new dirt road from Bear River to Spicy Breezes, and he'd cleaned up the trail from the mouth of Oil Creek on up to West Point. We had a freeway of fresh, graded dirt on which to move the cattle. Everyone knows that a cow will follow a fresh dirt road forever, right? As I believe Will Rogers said, "Sometimes what we know ain't so."

By the time we reached the mouth of Oil Creek, the heifers were very hot and very tired. They just refused to head up the hill. It was nearing the end of the day, and we struggled with them until dark. We finally succeeded in getting about seventy head to a pen at West Point near the shearing shed. All we could do then was give up 'til daylight.

The next morning, we found the remaining heifers lined up, head and tail, way up Oil Creek. The whole lot looked drawn, like gutted snow birds. It was obvious that as hot as they'd been, and in spite of standing in water all night, they had not taken a drink. They were in tough condition, but they were manageable. We put them with those already waiting at the shearing shed and headed the whole bunch on toward Central Park. As we moved across the Lower Eastern (once the lower, eastern part of the Russ Ranches, now actually the upper, western part of Andy's Central Park), we had the first heifer drop out. We left her and went on.

In that area, the ground was badly rutted. It had broken up as a result of movement during the winter; later on, the ground would dry and crack. It was also in this area that Lou Bugenig's horse stumbled and fell, taking Lou with it. The resulting injured knee kept Lou out of commission for a day or two.

The next morning, we headed up on what was part of Andy's new road, through Branstetters' Peters Place toward Spicy Breezes. As soon as we got into the timber, the cattle and horses were hit with a swarm of yellow jackets. We got through that all right but continued to have difficulty moving the cattle up the very steep road, and several more heifers dropped back before we reached the pens at the top of the ridge.

Over the next several days, we rode back to places where the cattle had dropped out, working to move them up. Amazingly, despite a few losses, nearly every heifer that made it to Spicy Breezes had a healthy calf later that fall.

By the end of the trip, the morale of the crew was pretty low. We weren't about to give up, however. We had a lot more cows to move from Fern Cottage to Bear River, and we thought it unlikely that hot weather would be a factor as we entered October. In addition, these cows didn't have as long a trip: They only needed to make it to Mazeppa. We were confident that with the experience we had gained, we could pull off a second attempt.

There was one obstacle, though, that we had no control over: the ocean. We planned to go about one month after our first attempt, so we would have a complete cycle of tides to deal with. When we rode to check the beach to make sure that we could get through the difficult areas, there was no beach. The waves had removed enough sand to make it impassible, even at the lowest tides.

It is said that Mother Nature bats last. It may also be that Mother knows best. We didn't make that last drive, and to my knowledge, no one else ever has either. That September 1980 effort was the last cattle drive between Ferndale and Bear River.

TRANSITIONS

It feels like California is always in a state of transition. These days we are watching the climate and the sociopolitical landscape change the cities and natural areas that make up our state. We are contending with evolving science and technology, as well as with human needs and the moral issues that come with change. And, as always, we make up diverse generations that are learning from each other, butting up against each other, and helping each other move into the next stages of our lives. Each generation has knowledge, traditions, and a collective ethos—and conflicts that arise as the children who are its heirs attempt to adapt to and address contemporary issues. These are the stories of people who have lived and are living through transitions affecting rangelands across the West.

Beneath All Is the Land

Jessica Schley

I belonged to that land. This is how I felt as a kid. It's how I still feel.

The ranch where you grow up, if you are lucky enough to grow up on one, stays with you forever. It is the most beautiful place you've ever seen, no matter where in the world you go. The green spring of your childhood is the greenest anywhere. The golden light at the end of a summer day is the most golden you've ever walked through, and the melody of a ranch evening is the most beautiful music to ever enter your ears, as the crickets trade verses in the grasses. *This never leaves you.* You never leave it, either. Even when you do.

In 2013 I wound down the ranch driveway for the very last time, the dust of the road rising up beneath my truck tires before settling back down in the washboards and potholes. This day marked the end of five generations of my family living and visiting there, for a total of eighty-six years—which is actually not much time compared to that of many ranching families. A coyote crossed the driveway on the way down the hill, and a white egret I'd never seen before flew off as the electric gate swung open to usher me out onto the main road. I stopped and chose a rock from the dry brook next to the driveway. It was the size of my open hand, sort of heart-shaped, with green and yellow moss. *My memento,* I thought to myself; my piece of the ranch that could always stay with me. A stone heart was perfect: it signified how my own heart felt at the time—numb, cold, and plucked out of, displaced from, the landscape where it had belonged.

A decade on, and I still wake up every night having dreamt of the ranch. I get up in the morning with the ranch in my forethoughts, as though there are chores still to go and do. It's not outside my front door anymore, but the ranch and chores are certainly always on the front porch of my mind, like a pleasant haunting.

I love that it haunts me, and I hope it never stops. It's painful, but it is full of love. It feels closer that way, as though it will be just tomorrow when we leave the ranch behind: before I open my eyes each morning when I wake up, for that little window of time, I'm still there at the ranch, for one more day.

And the brilliant greens and golds never change in the hauntings, in the daydreams, unlike the way the life before me constantly does. The ranch is always there, consistent and unwavering, with a stability it lacked in real life, but that's the beauty of dreams.

It took me years to learn that this feeling is called *hiraeth*, a Celtic word that means "longing for a place that you can never return to, either because it is no longer there or because it never was." There isn't a word for this in American English, and that surprises me so much, because in the four-hundred-plus years since we non-Indigenous Americans set foot on this continent, we've certainly experienced hiraeth a lot—and caused a lot of others to feel it too.

But perhaps it *is* significant that this concept does not exist in our language, as though the feeling is not important enough to belong to a word. The dominant theme of American culture has always been to look forward, to the next frontier, to the rugged horizon, to the future. Interesting, then, how much we glorify and gild our past. The past and the future: two extremes, and never enough time in the present moment, that place in between.

My life now is very different from what it could have been, what it would have been, if I and my cousins had become the next generation of stewards of the ranch. I am my grandmother's granddaughter, but I am not the woman whom a grandchild will one day look back at from up ahead on the trail, smiling from her saddle, the two of us out to check the cattle together on a gleeful spring day. I'm not ever going to wonder, while waving to that child as she rides up ahead, amazed by her fearless spirit, whether she would feel trapped by the burden of inheriting the ranch from me. Or question, alternatively, whether I was making the right decision in my will to have my heirs pack up and sell the land.

Deciding not to make a plan for the family to keep the ranch wasn't an easy decision for my grandmother, and I know that. I loved her like no one else, but do I resent her for that decision? Only as much as I do not understand what factors compelled her to make it. The pain of it all only makes the memories more vivid. The grass more emerald. The light more golden. The sunset more vermillion. The old, falling-down black-smith's shed with the hole in the roof, and the bellows still standing, more dreadfully synesthetic, with the taste of dust on my tongue and the rotten-wood smell in my nostrils and the feel of the cold, damp, metal anvil, gritty with moss and rust, under the palm of my hand. My entire heart is filled up with love for a ranch that I belonged to but which was never meant to belong to me.

I was not meant to be my grandmother. I was not meant to raise five boys during a world war, work cattle, fix fences, and worry about whether the well would run dry during a drought. The part of me that belonged to the ranch is the part of me that is behind, not in front. I came from a cattlewoman, and I became a cattlewoman's granddaughter. I became the last chapter, the land's end. I am so glad, and fortunate, to have been anywhere at all on that timeline, because the alternative is not to have known or been a part of the ranch at all.

"Beneath all is the land," begins the preamble to the Realtor Code of Ethics. That sentence electrified me when I first read it. Before I knew that it was the basis of all land-use law, I knew it was the truth of my life and of how my family's ranch became me. How the ranch formed and shaped and guided me. How it is, and always will be, underneath me.

And, because the universe loves a tragic joke, I'm a realtor now. Someone who helps land change hands, who helps direct a process between those leaving and those coming in, a transition that once held such a completely different connotation for me.

I used to hope to one day weave together my knowledge of ranching and land with my skill set in real estate. I said for years that my hope was to eventually combine my real estate career with conservation. I wanted this because I was still struggling with the juxtaposition of values that these two areas of my life seemed to have, and I didn't want to live a life of opposing values.

Just a week or two ago, I realized that somewhere in between the wishing forward and the looking back of the last decade since leaving the ranch, I had begun doing just that. I work with the California Rangeland Trust, as the Chair of their Legacy Council, which is a fitting name because our purpose is to help raise awareness and funds to preserve ranches, like the one I grew up on, for future generations so that

California can keep ranchers ranching, cattle grazing, and rangelands in production, for the health of our state as well as our world.

My life now is not the future I wanted for myself at age ten, when my dream was to be my gramma one day, but it's something I'm so glad to be dedicated to now. After leaving the ranch, I wasn't sure what purpose my life truly had any longer, if it wasn't to steward that land. Nita Vail, a good friend and founding Director of the Rangeland Trust, recognized that. She saw that I needed to regain a sense of purposefulness and also saw just how much danger I was in, drifting along alone, without a land anchor.

I wish I had never overheard the adults talking in the other room about what would become of the ranch one day, "when grandmother dies." I was ten. I shouldn't have been eavesdropping. All the same, it was a shock, and I couldn't fathom a life off the ranch. I ran outside to the barnyard and cried ugly tears at the anvil in the blacksmith's shed. That day, the charming, rustic outbuilding full of magic took on a different hue. The rust and the decay all around me meant something that it took me years to begin to understand and possibly still don't, not completely, anyway.

I have forged meaning out of my life with a blacksmith's tools from my childhood, stoked from a coke forge bellows and crucible that hadn't fired in decades. I hammered out a rudimentary set of ironclad beliefs against a silent anvil, so old and untouched by the time I was a little girl that a patina of rust and moss grew in a patchwork on its surface.

And today, as of this writing, I realize: a true, working ranch, one that is viable and that sustains its stewards, one that has stewards worthy of the job of sustaining it, doesn't have anvils that collect moss and tools that collect rust.

A working ranch has a smooth, black anvil that sings.

Motherland

HEATHER BERNIKOFF

Even if it is difficult, I want you to try something. Close your eyes; breathe deeply. If you catch the smell of tarweed—a hint of citrus, a touch of nectar, a bit of musk—if you catch just a little bit of warmed oak bark with pine sap and a gulp of soil, then a touch of cow pie, you just may be smelling love, breathing happiness.

Now listen: beyond the seemingly synchronized cow calls, a low-pitched whistle that hits high before trailing off—a soaring red-tail—and a cacophony of clicks, whistles, throatiness, mimicking, and movements from songbirds of every type. Buzzing, flitting, the sound of grass moving with the steady breeze as bees, tarantulas, and gophers make their way through the air and along the ground. There is the gentle crash of acorns falling from the trees. Then, off in the distance, or maybe closer if you have been very quiet on your walk, a high-pitched and undulating conversation of the coyotes. If you know the chord, you can start them singing or join in the canorous chorus.

Now feel the aromatic breeze across your cheeks, its scent sticking to you, the subtle hum of electricity that is the energy of life, tingling you with its joyful electrons. Finally, there is you, not separate, but a part of it all. They hear you, even the trees. They all know you are there. You are all together. Are you there, in the western foothills of the Sierra Nevada?

I did not start in this place. My family has not been on this land for generations. I started my life in a city. Even then, my mother saw it. She was a city girl, too, but we were the same. We had wild hearts. My mother was Yo'eme or, as the surrounding tribes named her people, Yaqui. Her people had been brought to Northern California as slaves to work the gold mines and, by the Bureau of Indian Affairs in partnership with big agricultural companies like the Dole Corporation, to pick crops. That had happened two generations before her time, and although you can take the Indian off the land, you cannot take the land out of the Indian. Mom saw that spirit in me: always finding a patch of greenery, an empty lot, a landscaped median, or our backyard as a place to nestle my body into the soil, make a living space, and talk to the crows, play with the spiders, watch the clouds float by.

When we moved from the city to the coniferous forests of the Sierra Nevada, it was no surprise to her that I would be gone all day, just me and my dog, with a bota bag of water and a sandwich in my pocket, exploring the woods, swimming in creeks, and wandering the deer trails. My mother explained to me that these were all my relations. We respected their life and they ours because we were, in fact, one. This is how I spent most of my youthful life, on the edge of the Stanislaus National Forest, falling deeper and deeper in love with land, my relation, its spiral helix entwined and fully integrated with mine.

Over time, I would see my land and animal relatives get pushed farther and farther away as surveyors' stakes pierced the ground and bulldozers felled trees and turned up the earth to make houses and stores. I did not understand. I had no power. I was a little girl—eventually a young woman. As I left for college, I promised myself that I would save as much land as I could when I grew up.

It was the tarweed that eventually stuck me to this ranch, but first it was my mother who brought me back home to the Sierra Nevada. She was ill. Diabetes, the ghost of colonization that haunts Native people, was changing her insides. It made her so sick. Despite the pills and plans, she was declining. I decided to come home to be nearer to her. I had married a really good guy who loved my mother and loved me. When I saw this ranch for sale an hour south of my parents' place, I knew he would think I was crazy. David is a city boy—and when I say city, I mean Los Angeles. But there was something about him: the fact that he was a camp counselor, the fact that he went as far away from L.A. as possible to go to a school built in a forest, a school where we met. There was a twinkle of country in him that made him willing to take this adventure with me. In the end, the tarweed, true to its name, also stuck him here to the land.

I helped my dad care for my mom, as I cared for the land, developing a relationship with my new home. The ranch was in disrepair. The house on the property was owner built and unfinished. Fencing was falling, garbage was everywhere. The people who were there before us had lost their connection with this place. The ranch was my project, so it was my job to make reparations, to improve our human relationship with the land. We are here for such a short time; how can we "own" anything but our choices? The hope is that we live in a good way, in reciprocity with, not domination over the land—a way that leaves it healthier than when we arrived so that future generations of all living things can thrive.

We inherited a cattleman with the ranch. He leased the ground for his cow-calf operation. He was old school. Men were in charge, and there was only one way to do things. We got along, but that was about it. Modern ranching is like quilting. As California parcels up all the wide-open spaces into smaller and smaller pieces, with many types of people "owning" them, cattlemen and women must increasingly sew together (via lease) additional places to make any kind of living. This means they must communicate, cooperate, and work with more and more people to keep up. Market consolidations, artificial supports for dairy, and ongoing drought have all made the cattle business tough.

Most of the family ranchers I know have other jobs or side businesses, and their spouses often work for the government or for a business that provides stability and health insurance. My inherited cattleman was from a different era. He did not have a side hustle. He did not like to talk to a lot of people. He did not want government handouts or the paperwork that came with them. He sure didn't like others knowing his business. He eventually filed for drought relief, had to share his personal business, had to talk to people like me and like those at the USDA Farm Service Agency. He found himself doing more and more of what he didn't want to do but *had* to do as ranching in California kept changing. He finally got out.

It is not just antitrust activities and drought that threaten ag producers; there is also the constant pressure of development. While developers have their place and can do their job well, few of them see an engaged community as an asset to work with. As a result, many ranchers find themselves involved in policy issues by necessity. Why? Even if you have a one-thousand-acre ranch, what happens upstream or adjacent to you will impact your operation, your livelihood. Precedents can be created that diminish ag rights, and before you know it, you are surrounded by tract homes, roving bands of domestic dogs, traffic, and people complaining about smells, sounds, and manure. Or worse, a mine operation moves next door, blasting, polluting the water that your cattle and family drink, causing cows to abort their calves, your family to get sick, and forcing that mating pair of golden eagles, who have lived by your side for years, to leave.

No one really wants to, nor has the time to, spend hours in government meetings, inform and organize community members, and then spend even more time researching each issue, but I had to. I had made a commitment to protect the land those many years ago. You can't afford to pay attorneys to do it, so it is up to you and, if you are lucky, maybe a handful of concerned neighbors. A county's General Plan is the guiding document for land-use planning. All decisions begin there, so you better know how to navigate it. Then there are Community or Town Plans, as well as zoning ordinances that dictate the implementation of the General and Community Plans, providing the teeth for enforcement. Then there are all the other agencies crucial for you to monitor: planning commissions, economic development commissions, water commissions, municipalities, and all the agendas and minutes generated by their meetings. They are all important. Exhausted yet? It is exhausting, especially when you are struggling to make some sense of what is being proposed, always on a tight timeline, and when you do not have the professional training to understand what you are looking at.

You can get worn out, and I did. My mother's health was declining. She required more care, more two-hour, round-trip drives north to her home. I took a break from being a lead in advocacy work to focus on her, my job, and the ranch. That was all I could fit in. Sometimes I would bring her to the ranch. She loved this place; I loved her. We would watch the dragonflies swarm, witness harriers perform their grid-like prey pursuits, sniff tarweed, listen to the coyotes, and look at the stars in the sky. It was a victory for her that I "owned" all this ground.

My grandfather felt the same way. He was a farmworker who ended up in the Bay Area after World War II. Before he came back to California, he tried to make a go of it in Nebraska, where his wife was from. He was denied loans to buy a piece of land despite having cash down, a job, and being a decorated combat veteran. The loan agents were racist. It was a systemic problem. No brown people were allowed to own land in certain parts of Omaha. My grandfather always remembered being treated like he was nothing. Like my mother, he was able to feel like our family had a chance through me. My ranch was a symbol of progress and achievement. We were moving ahead. He dreamed of building a little cottage on the ranch and planting a garden. It was a nice dream.

When my grandfather died in 2009 and my mother the year after, the land provided me a welcome respite from too much contemplation of what I had lost. The hills swaddled me, and the sounds helped soothe the pain. There is nothing better to remind you of the cycle of life than a ranch or farm. Life and death are all around you, and the scale of your home against the bucolic beauty of the undulating land, or beneath the mass winking of the starry sky, reminds you of how you are a small part of a much larger world connected with a million other people going through the same thing as you.

With the loss of my mother and the end of caregiving responsibilities that I had been honored to perform, I had a large hole in my spirit. Day by day, I felt it fill with love and light until I was whole again. It was a renewal of vigor, and I threw this nurturing energy into the land—both through advocacy and projects on the ranch. I had learned much about rangeland since I had first purchased the property and some about the cattle business. I had gained valuable experience trying out compost and implementing native and food plantings in the soil on a small scale. I had made good local friends, including some who were Indigenous and some in ag, and I now had time to learn more from them. Combining all of this with my strong science background and Indigenous values, I devoted greater time to this place, focusing even more intently on water, habitat, and soil.

Increasingly, the government entities that support ag were seeing the need to engage landowners and operators in ecosystem services that address climate change, habitat loss, and water and air quality. I was already working on soil moisture with a swale project and had planted a small section of native plants. I was ready to throw myself completely into this work and to be a small, but present, part of the solution.

Fortunately, there were several ag-focused agencies that increased the number of workshops they provided to teach best practices in a variety of aspects of agriculture. Being on their mailing lists helped me to learn about the trends and about what funding might be available. It was through my local Resource Conservation District (RCD) that I first learned of a grant program through the Wildlife Conservation Board and the California Association of RCDs that focused on improving pollinator habitat on rangeland.

I had read about the decimation of the monarch butterfly population. My ranch was in the flyway, and I wanted to help. I began by planting butterfly-attracting plants like milkweed and a variety of other nectar sources, but I was not able to scale up enough to help build back lost habitat. Working with my RCD, I was then able to win a pollinator grant. This gave me the opportunity to scale larger, and I will have planted more than one thousand plants, shrubs, and trees by the time this is published.

I have a new cattleman, who is a better match with me. He is younger and follows the science of grass and soil. He rotates the cattle aggressively, emulating the movement of the original, precolonial grass eaters that used to be here, like elk. My cattleman and I regularly discuss the timing and location of grazing during the monarch migration season. Working together, we are able to meet both our goals, which require healthy soil. The grazing helps to keep the nonnative grasses from outcompeting the native milkweeds, flowers, and other plants. A complex arrangement of branch and traditional fencing helps keep the cattle away from oak and willow seedlings, as well as from other plants that they would otherwise eat. We have seen improvement since implementing these changes and strategies: many more butterflies, ground-nesting birds, and plenty of grass. The ranch, and all my relations, are doing well.

Today, if she saw me as a middle-aged woman, my mother would find me much as I was as a child—outside, muddy, planting seeds, and dreaming. I see her in every tree, bird, and blade of grass. Indeed, the cells, blood, and bones of our ancestors help make up the soil, their own bodies having been made from the plants and animals, whose bodies were made from the soil. It is this soil on which we make a living, make a life, and make our food. The land cannot be contained, just as the monarch butterflies traverse from ocean to mountains to plains; just as the smell of tarweed travels through its sticky seed on the hide of all things; just as my mother's spirit is everywhere. The land is part of our family: let it be itself, and let us be grateful for its presence in our life.

Irrelevance Is No Longer
an Issue at the V6

Jack Varian

Going broke in the cattle business occurs for several reasons. Some of these reasons are outside a person's control, for instance, an extended drought or maybe a huge dump in the cattle market, where holding on by the skin of your teeth has come and gone, and your banker says, "Sorry." Then there's the slower kind of going broke, when the ranch owner— without even knowing it until it's too late—becomes irrelevant due to his unwillingness to accept changing times.

I believe that was almost my lot in life, but I was saved by a phone call from a friend and neighbor who made me aware of a seminar in my shopping town, Paso Robles, California. He invited me to a gathering called Holistic Resource Management, where I would hear of a new way to make better decisions about how to manage my ranch. The year was 1991, and after three days of eye-opening alternatives to going broke, I gave myself permission to do things differently.

It was one of those "easy to say" but not quite so "easy to do" things. My wife, Zee, and I had been doing things a certain way since we got to the V6 Ranch in 1961. My new religion now required me to test my old methods and to throw them out if they didn't pass muster. My cavalier attitude started to evaporate when I told myself that I was really going to replace old "familiar" with the "unknown." As one successful change was followed by another, however, it got easier. Finally, I said to myself, "Jack, I wish you had discovered this new path to free and original thinking sooner."

I started dabbling with a few ways of doing things differently, like rejuvenating the Little Cholame Creek, a seasonal stream dotted with old

cottonwood trees but with no new ones taking seed in the last one hundred years. I decided to keep my cattle out of the creek in the spring and
summer months. Nineteen ninety-two was a pretty good year for rain,
and by July there were new cottonwoods coming up all along six miles of
the creek. Now the ranch has a creek whose banks are, for the most part,
stable, and I like to think it looks today as it might have looked two hundred years ago. It was very rewarding to the strings of my heart, but this
effort didn't pay many bills. Little did I know how shortsighted my vision
of the future was.

One summer eve, Zee and I came out of our local movie theater after
seeing a very enjoyable film about three middle-aged guys who go on a
cattle drive. The movie was called *City Slickers*, and it starred Billy Crys-
tal. I looked at Zee and said, "We can do that. We have the ranch, all the
horses you have trained, thirteen trophy saddles, and a whole lot of tack
that you've won. Let's give it a go." And go we did: by October 2023, we
had finished our twenty-seventh year of offering annual cattle drives to
city slickers.

"Jack, who are you at this minute?" I think that's a fair question, or
better yet, "What have you become since that holistic meeting in 1991?"
My answer is that I'm a cattleman who has morphed into a grass man
who harvests sunlight. That means I sell sunlight: it produces the grass I
use to feed my beef cattle, all while making the ranch better because of
holistic grazing. I raise beautiful landscapes for the good of my soul and
for our new, number-one industry, "agritourism," a most amazing new
way to do things with endless possibilities for the twenty-first century.

You can't do any of this without water. For the past seven or eight
years, the V6 has had an extensive water-distribution system stretching
to all parts of the land, thanks to a product called poly pipe. With this
system in place, all the cattle, horses, and wildlife have many places to
live their lives because they can always find food, water, and places to
hide. The grass and shrubs also prosper because they are more evenly
grazed.

But what good is Camelot if it is only for a moment in time? There
must be some sort of ongoing protection for the livestock and the wildlife, and that costs money. Part of the answer is to protect the lives of
game animals by having a hunting club with thirty members. "Jack," you
might be saying, "killing game animals you hope to save sounds like a
perfect definition of an oxymoron." Yet, this is where money talks, for

when you give something economic value, this value guarantees that it can prosper. The long-term goal for wildlife and livestock is for their numbers to prosper until each reaches a Mother Nature-approved compatible population.

The holistic model came through again for me in 2000. I was dry farming close to one thousand acres of grain hay with a full complement of bailers, swathers, disks, tractors, and more, which guaranteed a trip to town every day for the repair parts needed to keep this destructive and fertility-robbing soil degradation going. This was something I had been doing since our arrival in 1961. Something in my brain was starting to say, "Baling up all this hay every year doesn't make any sense. But Jack, everybody bales hay every year in May. They can't all be wrong."

Still, there was just enough doubt in my mind that—with a fair amount of trepidation—I decided to see if making dry-land grain hay the way I always had passed the holistic test. It failed miserably. Disking the soil is one of the most destructive and erosive cultural practices there is. The real eye-opener came when I added up all the costs of making hay. I could buy it from my neighbor more cheaply than I could raise it. It was pretty easy to convince myself that buying was better than raising. But I wanted to make sure I wouldn't relapse into the old ways, so I sold my mountain of iron equipment, and with my oxyacetylene torch, I cut a perfectly good road grader up into little pieces and sold it for scrap. My commitment was complete. "Dear soil, rest easy. This won't happen again while I'm in command."

Perhaps the most important accomplishment for Zee and me was placing a conservation easement over the entire ranch in 2001. I firmly believe that with the placement of the easement, we did away with the usual family turmoil and hate over who receives an inheritance because there's nothing to divide. The one avenue left is to be good stewards of the land. And by giving the ranch to the Varian Family LLC that our four children co-own, we are making sure that there will be no inheritance tax to pay. I think the V6 has a very good chance of lasting for a very long time. Just think how reassuring it would be to all the critters above and below the soil surface to know that they're never going to be homeless.

"Jack, you mean you no longer own the V6?!" That's right, Zee and I are now tenants who have a life estate in our house and who rent the grazing land for our cattle business from our children.

Zee and I are blessed with having no regrets about choosing this way to lead our lives, even though we grew up as "city kids." We're a testament to the fact that where you are raised has nothing to do with what you will be good at. Once you have an inkling of where you will fit into the working world, passion and risk-taking will determine how good you are going to be at your chosen profession. Mine just happens to be cattle ranching.

There will always be a need for cowboys, cowgirls, and cow horses because there are an awful lot of mountains in the West that only a horse can take you over. Cow people who like people will always have work to do in passing their trade on.

This organic movement is no flash in the pan. It's here to stay. So, to all of you who want to own a piece of this bounty's pie, turn your imaginations loose. Become an observer of everything, and then read anything and everything, for you never know when some obscure bit of information might lead you in a new direction. If you have truly picked the right occupation, most of the time it won't seem like work at all.

A Few Generations Down the Line

LAUREN VARIAN

Seven and a half years ago, inspired by the kind of wanderlust you get from growing up in a town of eighteen people, paired with a passion for music, I moved to Ireland for college. I was lucky to be welcomed with open arms.

I'm Jack and Zee Varian's second-oldest grandchild, Lauren. I'm writing at the tail end of the infamous year 2020, and I've been weathering the global pandemic on the west coast of Ireland in a small village called Strandhill.

In these few years, I've been given the opportunity to work with my heroes, doing what I can to share and to document the culture and music that I've grown to love so dearly. It's been wildly different from my childhood, which has been an exciting challenge and gift. But as the years have gone on, my ache for home has grown harder and harder to ignore. It's become clear to me that the most important work I can do in my life is to protect the V6 Ranch as best I can, and I can't do a very good job of that from five thousand miles away. So, in 2021 my Irish boy and I will head west, back to the V6.

The ranch provided me with the best childhood imaginable. When I was born, my Grandpa Jack was a recent convert to the practice of holistic management. Later, on childhood hikes with Grandpa, we'd celebrate the fruits of this shift in thinking and the labor that went into it: once-dry creeks running again, wildlife populations growing and diversifying, rings of mushrooms returning to what were formerly tired hay fields, and more. Grandpa would teach us how to install gravity-fed troughs and to kick dry cow pies to help them break down, while Grandma Zee taught us horsemanship skills on her line of horses. As a teenager I worked as a wrangler on trail rides that my parents organized and through which they taught thousands of people from all walks of life about *our* way of life. As an adult, seeing the ranch after months away is healing and mind-bogglingly beautiful. I am immensely lucky to have grown up learning to respect the land and its creatures.

Looking to the future, I'm filled with nervous excitement about the opportunity to combine the skills and perspectives I've gained in Ireland with the lessons that my family and the land have to teach me. I'm optimistic that my perspective will help me question more and take less for granted, will help me keep the ranch prepared for an uncertain and rapidly changing future. Most importantly, these seven-plus years away have given me an appreciation for my home that I may not have fully realized if I had stayed at home. Here's to the future!

Slán go foil ("Goodbye for now").

La Chapelle de Madrone

JESSICA SCHLEY

You said the land is like your church.
The dirt you find the bear tracks in
means as much to you
as the tracks do, themselves.

I crossed myself as I watched you
because I had entered your sacred ground,
and I must observe carefully, your traditions.

The canyons are chapels,
filled thick with rows of worshippers on
pews of manzanita, madrone, bay trees.
Sagebrush pays homage low to the ground,
silently praying to a god unknown.

There are stained-glass
windows in your church
that stare back like rock faces
on mountainsides, with waterfalls
plummeting hundreds of feet.

Secret vestibules are hidden
behind tapestries of green brush
twenty feet tall. They will stay hidden
until a hellfire rakes the altar cloths
from their sacrificial hiding places.

Grisaille frescoes run at our feet
in the form of grey creek beds on
either side of the rutty, old road,
which is the center aisle to
the altar mountain.

Baptisms have been held here,
funerals, weddings,
births and deaths.
Bovine congregations have gathered
at the baptismal fountain
high in the mountains where the cold
springs flow. They have witnessed the ancient
covenant of blessing new life found here and
forgiving it of sins which it has not yet committed.

The river has wiped away the trespasses of generations;
the pond has collected years of family homestead memories.
Reflection into its murky depths brings about
more questions than silent answers.

Indians are buried ceremoniously beneath
long boulders, placed over their graves with
long levers and pulls, and human sweat and blood
commitment placed them carefully in their eternal ground.

Blue soapstone bowls are the most prized treasure to be found
in the earth here. They are communion donations from the
forefathers of this church. It was called *Nojoqui,*
and the word has lost its meaning, but for the land
which now holds that name.

I watch you bend down in the aisle of your church.
Facing the high mountain altar, staring down at the
bear track, taller than your own palm. You kneel with
one hand on a pew as if in observation of high Episcopal
custom, and bow your head to the mountain before you rise
to walk in the steps of the bear's footprints.

You said the land is like your church.
I crossed myself as I watched you kneel.

A Funny Story

LINDA STANSBERRY

The first time I knew we were different? It might have been one rainy morning on the drive to school. It rains a lot where I'm from—or it used to, before climate change began flexing its muscle—big, loud storms that can send the river spilling over its banks and across the county road. In the 1980s and 1990s, before cell phone coverage was ubiquitous, almost everyone in the Mattole Valley had a CB radio, and on winter mornings when the storms were especially vicious, my little brother and I would listen eagerly against the static for the announcement that a culvert had washed out and school was canceled.

If the progress of time is a stream, then the place where I'm from is an eddy, just a little slower and wilder than everywhere else. It may have been that wildness that brought the tourists to the county road—the same one I spent two hours traveling on every day to get to school—but I doubt they were anticipating the full vigor of a West Coast storm, one fierce enough to throw a giant Douglas-fir across the road.

We were prepared. A rancher is always prepared. Every vehicle we owned, even the steadfast Suburban that bused us to school and softball games, was essentially a rolling toolbox, with bows of baling twine in the glove compartment and everything you'd need to rope a steer, fix a fence, or repair a watering trough somewhere on the floor. The rain on this morning was coming down in sheets, so it was tough at first to see why the car in front of us had stopped, but its driver got out and, bearing a purple umbrella, came back to tell my dad that he couldn't move the tree.

I must have been about nine or ten, and I remember feeling everything a child should feel at that age as my father calmly went to the back of the truck and took out his chainsaw. He must have been wearing his oiled, waterproof duster and his felt cowboy hat, his winter clothes. I felt great pride in my father, in his capability, in his readiness for everything.

I felt comforted by my mom, who knew I had another hour or so to ride on the school bus and so wouldn't let me get out to help and get my school clothes wet. And I felt the interior smirk of a family joke form as we watched the tourist waffle helplessly in the road, finally dashing through the rain to hold the umbrella above my father's head as he worked.

I had always thought the humor in this story was self-evident, but I was wrong.

"You see, it's funny because in the country we don't use umbrellas," I tried telling my city friends, who were confused. But that wasn't quite it.

"And the guy held an umbrella over my dad while he cut the tree and moved it out of the road," I explained to my country friends. But they were mostly annoyed.

"Why didn't the tourist help move the log?" they asked. Good question.

The story is a funny story mostly to other dualists like me: to my friend who grew up in Seattle and then married a rancher; to my hippie friend with her urban homestead. They've hailed cabs and baled hay. They get it.

In 2014, just north of here, a family took a wrong turn down a logging road and got lost. They stayed in the car for a while, idling the engine and trying to keep the kids warm. After several days the father left on foot to get help. He froze to death sixteen miles away. Rescuers found his wife and children alive two days later. I think of that story often, and sometimes I try to express what it means, or what it means to me. It's not a funny story, and that's kind of the point. Nature has no sense of humor, just ironies that we assign her as we try to weave a narrative from her ceaseless arc.

Ranchers and those of us who live close to the land know this. We've got our own purple umbrellas, stories we hold over our heads to keep us safe. We sing along to country songs about love that's deeper than the holler and wild as a river flowing free. We put a chainsaw in the back of the family car and tell ourselves that we're ready for anything. When we witness the first rain of the year as it raises a faint green fuzz on the hills or discover that a new cow dog turns out to be a header, we praise what she—nature—gives us. When weather defies our plans to fix a fence or to catch a horse, we laugh as though she's in a conspiracy with us, nature, a prankster giving us our due. But, deep down, we know that it's not true.

I think of that family in the cocoon of the car, so confident, when they started their journey, in their belief that if a road was there, it must be safe. I don't think they were blunderers, or foolhardy. I think they were like that tourist with his purple umbrella, so used to living apart from nature that they forgot her eternal truth. She wins. She always wins. She might welcome you home in a deadfall at twenty, a wildfire at thirty, cancer at fifty, a heart attack at eighty, but she always wins. She'll pull down your barn, send grasshoppers for your hay, put an ache in your favorite dog's back legs. Nature doesn't care about roads or plans or families or whether or not you paid your crop insurance. She always wins.

"This is not a funny story," you're probably saying.

No. Yes. Humor's not where you find it, it's when you find it, and the sooner you find it, the better. Because nature's kicking us all in the teeth right now. She's putting brackets of wrinkles around my eyes, rerouting the stream I bermed last winter, guaranteeing that that ewe will start lambing in the mud around midnight on Christmas Day. She'll always win in the end. But she can't have all the things we mortals can have— wonder and humor and the swell of a child's pride, the hopefulness of a purple umbrella. She's better. She'll win. But, oh, we can laugh.

RESILIENCE

The relative comforts of modern life have not shielded us from the need to be resilient. Climate change has yielded devastating fires and droughts. Our capacity to provide energy, food, and homes has been tested. Social media and technologies threaten to distance us from our neighbors. Those who manage to live off the land have always had a tenuous existence. Their ability to adapt, survive, and thrive is especially crucial in the twenty-first century, and in these stories, they share those experiences and the lessons learned along the way.

I Cry for the Mountains
and the Legacy Lost

David A. Daley

It is almost midnight. We have been pushing hard for eighteen to twenty hours every day since the Bear Fire tore through our California mountain cattle range on September 8, 2020, and there is so much swirling in my head, I can't sleep anyway. The fire destroyed our range, our cattle, and, even worse, our family legacy. Someone asked my daughter if we had lost our family home. She told them, "No, that would be replaceable. This is not!" I would gladly sleep in my truck for the rest of my life to have our mountains back.

I am enveloped by overwhelming sadness and grief and then anger. I'm angry at everyone and no one. Grieving for things lost that will never be the same. I wake myself weeping almost soundlessly. And it is hard to stop.

I cry for the forest, the trees and streams, and the horrible deaths suffered by the wildlife and our cattle. The suffering was unimaginable. When you find groups of cows and their baby calves that have tumbled into a ravine, trying to escape, burned almost beyond recognition, you try not to retch. You only pray that death was swift. A fawn and small calf side by side, as if hoping to protect one another. Worse, in searing memory, cows with their hooves, udders, and even legs burned off who had to be euthanized. A doe lying in the ashes with three fawns, not all hers, I bet. And you are glad they can stand and move, even with a limp, because you really cannot imagine any more death today. Euthanasia is not pleasant, but sometimes it's the only option. But you don't want more suffering. How many horrible choices have we faced in the past three days?

We have taken cattle to the Plumas National Forest since before it was designated as such. It is a steep and vast land of predominantly mixed conifers and a few stringer meadows on the western slope of the Sierra Nevada, straddling Butte and Plumas Counties. My great-great-grandfather started moving cattle to the high country sometime after 1852, when he settled in the Oroville area looking for gold. The earliest family diary entry about driving cattle to our range in the mountains dates back to 1882: We were poor Irish immigrants trying to scratch a living from the land.

The range is between the south fork and middle fork of the Feather River, the drainage that fills Lake Oroville. It is eighty-inch-rainfall country from October to May, with deep snow at the high end, and then it goes completely dry. Three major streams/rivers and hundreds of creeks and springs punctuate the land. My friends from the arid West can't understand why it is hard to gather—"Don't you just go to the water?" Not that simple in this environment. It is difficult country, in some ways more suited to sheep because of the browse, but politics and predators killed the sheep industry in the country years ago. But the cows love the range and do well: cool days and nights, no flies, higher elevations avoiding the hot summers of the valleys. A great place to summer cattle. They actually like to go as much as we do!

For those of you who have never seen this land, this isn't riding a horse into a meadow or open ridge where you can see cattle. This is literally hunting through a vast forest of deep canyons, rivers and creeks, and the high ridges in between. It is not an easy place to gather or even to find cattle in the best conditions.

There are six generations of my family who have loved this land, and my new granddaughter, Juni, is the seventh. And I find myself overcome with emotion as I think of the things she will never see but will only hear about in stories told by her granddad. We all love the mountains. They are part of us, and we are part of them. All destroyed. In one day. I am angry.

As a child in the early sixties, our days of "going to the mountains" were the greatest ever for my family. It was our playground and our quiet spot. Sure, we worked, but we learned so much about the world, trees, birds, and flowers. And in my family, sometimes that included learning the scientific name or at least the family of the plant. There were lessons on botany, forestry, geology, archaeology. We didn't even know we were learning, but we imbibed it until it became a part of our souls.

And then my kids: For them, the mountains were the best! Rolling into a little seat behind Grandma and Grandpa to "go hunt for cows" as we gathered in the fall. Hot chocolate from Grandma as soon as we got there. On cold, dusty, or wet days, it was sometimes discouraging, but they loved it and still do. It was their sanctuary, where "no matter what happens, this will always be here." And now it is gone. It is a death, and we are still in shock and not sure how to move forward. What will my granddaughter know of the truth and grounding that come from nature? Will we gather cows in the mountains while I sing cowboy tunes off-key and she sips hot chocolate? I am overcome.

When the news broke of the fire in our cattle range, my son Kyle, who ranches with me, and I were sure it could not be as bad as it sounded. We had close to four hundred cows, most of them calving or close to calving, in our mountain range, and they would be ready for us to gather and bring them home in early October. They were the heart of the herd. Old cows, problematic ones, recently purchased cows, and first-calf heifers stayed in the valley. Only the good cows who knew the land were there.

That first day, we had no access and were relying on spotty reporting posted to local news or social media. My daughter, Kate, a veterinarian who practices about four hours away, said, "I'm on the way." My youngest son, Rob (named for his grandad), who is a soldier stationed in Louisiana, said, "I have a lot of leave, and I'm on a plane tomorrow." All three of my children are unbelievable, and we all need each other to navigate this heartbreak.

At first, we couldn't get into the range and were frantic as it was completely locked down because of safety concerns. We knew cattle were dying as we waited. I received a call from a Pennsylvania number and answered before thinking. A wonderfully nice man from the Forest Service was calling to tell me about the fire since I had a cattle allotment in the Bear Fire area. I had to help him find it on the map! Frustrating. And he knew less than I did. Later I got a call from San Bernardino (five hundred miles south), from another fire-resource officer with the Forest Service. I asked about access. "Well," he said, "maybe next week and only if we provide an escort. We have to make it safe first." He, too, had no idea where the allotment was or about the challenge that I faced. All the cattle would be dead if I waited a week. I politely told him I would figure out an alternative—through private timberland and common sense!

I called our county sheriff, who has been a great friend of the cattle community. I had to wait one day, but he provided two sergeants to help me navigate the roadblocks until I was in the range. Was it dangerous?

Yes. Were animals dying? Absolutely. Local solutions are always better, though. I am thankful to Sheriff Kory Honea, of Camp Fire and Lake Oroville Dam-breach fame, and to Sergeants Angelo Tavelli and Matthew Calkins, who got us access, all incredible people who get it. Local.

On our first day in, Kyle and I made a fast trip up to reconnoiter. We were unprepared for the total destruction of everything we had always known. Nothing left, and active flames on both sides burning trees and stumps. Shocking. Surreal. We made it to our Fall River corral somewhat hopeful that there would be greenery and water to mitigate the disaster. Everything was completely gone, and we saw dead cows as we started down the hill. Everywhere. This was our first step in what would be an impossible week. We went home hoping against hope that we had seen the worst. Little did we realize that it was just the beginning and that it could get worse.

Then it was 3:30 in the morning on day two, time to start this nightmare again. To find the courage to throw some things in the truck, run with the kids to check and feed the survivors, and hit repeat. I dreaded it but knew we must. And I worked to be optimistic because that is who I am. Not easy.

As we made a plan and split up to run four-wheelers up and down logging roads hunting for life and death, I thought about how lucky I was. So many people had offered to help. I was grateful, but it was difficult to explain how challenging it would be to gather in almost ninety thousand acres of incredibly difficult terrain (and that's on a flat map!). Each canyon and ridge was dotted with logging spur roads that could be choked with fallen and burning trees. Much of it would be unrecognizable, even to me. Only those with deep, local knowledge of these mountains could help. Fortunately, my family, the Carter boys (Devin and Doyle), Brian Jones—all friends of my kids and now friends of mine— plus my best friend, Sean Earley, all stepped up. They knew the mountains well and had helped us for years. They just showed up and said, "We're here. We're going. What can we do?" So, we strapped chainsaws and some alfalfa on four-wheelers and set out hoping against hope to find something alive.

We split up, and my crew took the Lava Top and Ross Creek drainage, while the other half went toward Twin Bridges and Fall River. It was eerie, and as Rob said, there was "no sound in the forest, just death." We were learning. When we traditionally gather our cows, they are always grazing toward the ridge top in the morning and down by the water in the afternoon. But on this day, we found nothing high up, except the occasional dead cow who wasn't fast enough. We just hunted for the deep holes where there was a chance of finding water and life.

You learned as you rode through the apocalyptic murk. Rob's head went up, and I caught the scent at the same time. The scent of death and charred flesh mingled with the acrid smoke that burned your eyes. You began looking in the draws, hoping not to see cattle. You always did. Eight cows and three baby calves in a pile at the bottom of a ravine, who rushed in terror to escape. A sight you wouldn't soon forget.

But that day, when we met up, Kyle and Kate had great news: They had found sixteen head at our Twin Bridges corral! The largest group to date. I had baited it with alfalfa last night, and there were cattle standing in the little corral of temporary panels. Remarkable. Two of them were heifers that I had given to Kyle and Jordan (my daughter in-law and Juni's mom) for their wedding. Kyle had branded them with my dad's original brand just to keep them straight. Someone in our crew said that Dad had gathered them for us so we wouldn't miss them. Maybe he had. My dad was a cow whisperer who has been gone over four years after roaming the mountains for almost ninety. Maybe he was still helping lead us and the cattle home. I turned away as I felt emotion begin to rise. Again. For some reason, I was more emotional when I found the live cattle than when I found those who had died. I didn't know why. Maybe thinking about what they had gone through and that I hadn't been there to help? And, more frightening, that death had become more expected than life.

I completely dread taking my mom to see this tragedy. She will be ninety in less than a month and still loves the mountains and gathering cows. She is tough, but this could break anyone. She worked these mountains with my dad from 1948 on, starting when she was eighteen, he was twenty-one, and they had just married. She told me in later years that she had always loved the outdoors but really was "sort of afraid of cows" since she had not ever been around them when she was young. She never told Dad, though, and learned to be one of the best trackers and gatherers the mountains have ever seen, knowing every plant, tree, and road.

You can learn more from old people. They may not use PowerPoint or Zoom. They may not talk about politics elegantly, but they have life experience. We are quickly losing their vital perspective about the land before allowing them to teach us. Their views are far more valuable than those of a visiting scholar or great consultant. They have local knowledge and observational skills. I wish we would listen.

I am, again, angry at everyone and no one. Why did this happen? I am absolutely tired of politicians and politics, from both the left and the right. *Shut up*. You use tragedies to fuel agendas and raise money to feed egos. I am sick of it. And it plays out on social media and cable news with distorted half-truths. *On both sides*. Washington, D.C., is three thousand miles away and is filled with lobbyists, consultants, and regulators who wouldn't know a sugar pine from a fir. Sacramento is one hundred miles south and feels even more distant than D.C. And to the regulators who write the *Code of Federal Regulations*, the policies and procedures, and then debate the placement of a comma: You mean well, I know. And I am sure you are good people. But you are useless when it comes to doing things to help the land. And as to the "nonprofits" (yeah, right), lawyers, and academics: This is all too often a game for you to play as you try to successfully navigate your own institution. "How do I get a grant to study something that I should realize, if I looked closely, generations before me already knew?" Nothing happens on the ground to make change. I do, though, understand that most folks truly care and start with the best intentions.

For those of you on the right who want to blame the left and California: These are National Forest lands that are "managed" by the feds. They have failed miserably over the past fifty years. Smokey Bear was the cruelest joke ever played on the western landscape, a decades-long campaign to prevent forest fires that has resulted in recent megafires of a scope we've never seen. Thanks, Smokey.

The U.S. Forest Service is constantly threatened with litigation from extremists who don't want anyone to use the forest: It is to be preserved. Great job in helping to get us where we are. And I feel bad for Forest Service personnel. Most of them are great people who work there because they love the land like I do. But they are chained to desks to write reports and to follow edicts handed down from those who don't know. One-size-fits-all regulations are not a solution in diverse ecosystems. And the Forest Service budget is consumed by fire suppression and litigation. What funds are left to actually work on the land?

And, for those of you on the left who want to blame it all on climate change: The regulations at the state and federal level have crippled—no, stopped—any progress toward changing the unmitigated disasters facing our landscapes. I wonder how many of you have walked the canyons or ridges or seen the wildlife and beauty at a secret stream?

Politicians stage drive-by photo ops to raise money from the fringes. None of us really like you. We are just forced to deal with you. Of course, there are many exceptions, and you know who you are. I hate to visit an office to discuss issues when the legislator is far more interested in talking than in listening. It seems that nobody can be a centrist and make sense and win. There is plenty of blame to go around on both sides of the aisle.

And just maybe it's both—horrible forest management and climate change. Don't you think months of massive smoke covering the West may impact the climate, especially when added to our other pollutants? Does it matter which came first? Why not invest in solutions rather than using sound bites to gin up the base? Locally, we know the solutions. And those investments should be locally conceived and locally driven.

I grew up hearing the stories from my dad and grandad of the "last man out" lighting the forest floor to burn the low undergrowth. Their generations knew how to reduce the ladder fuels that spread the fire to the canopy, to open it up for the wildlife. It was a pact shared between our friends, the Native Americans who had managed it this way for thirteen thousand years, and the loggers, miners, and ranchers. They knew ecology and botany and wildlife. They worked together because they loved and knew the land.

I remember a December in the early 1960s, when snow was already on the ground on our foothill ranch. I would have been about four and holding my grandfather's hand as he lit some piles of brush on fire to open up the landscape. It was the practice he had learned from generations of ranchers before him. And the CDF (now CAL FIRE) crew showed up, put out the fire, and lectured him about burning the brush. My grandad was the kindest, gentlest, and funniest man I have ever known. And he was mad. It was the beginning of the end for our forest home. And it has proceeded at an unprecedented rate.

I am angry. Try to conduct a controlled burn in the winter now, and watch someone cite you because it is not an approved "burn day," or you have the wrong approval permit, or you might impact air quality. It is beyond moronic. How is the choking air quality that has blanketed the West recently, preventing people from going outside without a mask, a better alternative? Are you kidding me? Bureaucrats and well-intentioned regulators have tied our hands, and the blame is shared at both the state and federal levels.

Lest you think that I am a complete rube: I earned my PhD in animal science thirty-five years ago at Colorado State. I loved teaching and ranching—so I did both. But I am a cattleman at heart. And I have been involved in industry activities for many years, serving as past president of the California Cattlemen's Association, as current chair of the California Cattle Council, as chair of the Forest Service committee for the Public Lands Council, and as chair of the National Cattlemen's Beef Association Federal Lands Committee. I have walked the halls of Congress and met with legislators in both Sacramento and D.C., and I am willing to advocate for the cattle community by reaching out to anyone who will listen. I have dined with legislators in D.C., Chicago, and Sacramento at wonderful restaurants noted for fine dining. The company, food, and conversation were enjoyable. And I have had bologna sandwiches and beer in the mountains with ranchers and loggers. Somehow, the air seemed cleaner, and the food was better with the latter. Something about straightforward honesty and hard work is appealing.

I invite any legislator or regulator, state or federal, to come with me to see this devastation. Leave your photographer behind, put on your boots, and let's go. I will buy the bologna. We have created tragedy after tragedy across the West, and we need solutions.

Look at the megafires that California has experienced in recent years. If you study them closely, almost all of them start on state or federally owned land. Fifty percent of California is owned by the feds or state, land that has unmanaged fuel loads because of restrictions on doing anything on the land. Right now, the only buffer to these disasters consists of private, well-managed, grazed landscapes: Fires may still burn there, but they are not as catastrophic and can be controlled. As for the megafires: Butte County alone had the Camp Fire in 2018, which destroyed the town of Paradise, population twenty thousand, and where almost one hundred people died. And now the Bear Fire caused an even higher percentage of deaths in Berry Creek, a small community of about one thousand residents, where fourteen people lost their lives.

Our segmented view of the landscape has led us to tragedy after tragedy. As a rancher in the forest, I am required, in the name of ecosystem health, to monitor meadow utilization, the browsing of willows by livestock and wildlife, and stream-bank alteration. Fine. I comply. If I hit 41 percent meadow utilization, I can get a letter of noncompliance since 40 percent is considered the maximum. The Bear Fire—as I would come to learn—would not leave 60 percent of the meadow! I wonder: Will I get a letter of noncompliance?

It is not the Forest Service ranger or conservationist's fault that I have to monitor these three factors. It's the fault of the guidelines they are handed, arbitrary and ineffective measures to protect the environment that are of no use against decades of unmitigated fuel growth. Can anybody look up and see the meadows and water disappearing? Is the health of the meadow crippled by unchecked understory growth that sucks the water out and allows invasion of conifers? It is easier to blame the cow. Look up. Watch nature. She will talk to you.

I think it is as simple as not seeing the forest for the trees. And in my earlier academic life, that was also the norm. I worked with wonderful faculty, staff, and students who were committed to research and teaching. However, we rarely looked at the big picture because we were encouraged to publish in our disciplines without seeking out how our work connected with other researchers' efforts or considering how our small piece was part of a larger solution. That siloed thinking plagues most bureaucracies and agencies. We only know what we know. And, in most disciplines in the academy, most faculty are now several generations removed from a direct connection with the land.

Listen to the generations who came before. Megafires are a recent product of failing to use fire prudently, of too little grazing, and of overregulation. And these catastrophic fires contribute to climate change. Yet the guidelines followed by the feds and by the state are one size fits all. It is beyond dumb. And no one's fault. And everyone's fault. Listen to the forest. Listen to the locals.

The fire in Santa Rosa in 2018 was estimated to produce more CO_2 and pollutants in one week than all the cars in California did in one year. We had six of the largest twenty fires in California history in 2020. The Bear Fire, as I would eventually learn, would end up burning more than 250,000 acres. To me this is very personal, but this is a much bigger problem than my family losing our cattle.

I get frustrated with experts and consultants who drive by and know just what to do. For thirty-five years I have attended conferences, given presentations, and listened. What I have learned is that solutions are local and specific. What happens in one watershed in Plumas or Butte County may be entirely different in Lassen National Forest just next door. But experts of all kinds are glad to tell you how to do it. "Let's prescribe graze, use virtual fences, change your timing, change your genetics." Prescribe graze the forest and canyons? Yeah, right. They don't know what they don't know, but they will take the honorarium anyway and have a great dinner on your dime. Another game where the people who live here and the land rarely benefit.

I have traveled and given presentations nationally and internationally for decades as the odd academic cowman. I learned quickly that it is insulting to make suggestions if you don't know the land, the people, and the culture. I don't love those canned "you should do this and do that" PowerPoint talks. They are frustrating. My approach has always been: "This is what I do and why—it may not fit here so don't force it." I loved those trips, not because of what I taught but because of what I learned from the locals.

Cattle, like the wildlife, follow the season in this wildland we love. They start at low elevation in June and work east and higher until early October. As leaves begin to change, they start west and down. How and why would you fence this land? Again, an expert from afar who wrote a text or managed a ranch in a different ecosystem might think this is a great idea. It is exhausting.

Now, by day four, I have come to understand what first responders mean when they say "rescue to recovery." I hold out little hope for live cattle. We have to get to Hartman Bar Ridge between the middle fork and south branch of the Feather River. It's the part of the range that is the farthest north, the most breathtaking, and the hardest to access. One road in and one road out, choked with downed and sometimes burning trees. We see a burnt bear cub trying to climb a tree, and two miles farther along, a mature bear, burnt but staying in the water, trying to ease the pain. We give them both a chance because they have made it this far. We won't euthanize them even though our brains say we should. Our hearts say, let them try.

We have about six miles of road to make passable to get stock trailers through, but we make short work of it. Sometimes you can travel a quarter mile and sometimes one hundred feet. But chainsaws and strong hands get us there.

I pass several streams and try to wade across one looking for cattle. It strikes me as strange. All the creeks have close to double the flow of last week's. I see some springs running that haven't been active for years. And then it hits me: We have released the water that the brush was sucking from the land. The Native Americans were right again. Observe. Let nature talk.

We pull up the grade to Hartman Bar Ridge and Whiskey Hill, and there are cattle tracks in the burn! Lots of them. I can't believe it. The fire roared up out of the middle fork so quickly that I expected nothing to be alive. I had myself prepared. But we find cattle, and some in pretty good shape. It is slow going. Incredibly steep and rugged, with lost, hungry cattle. In one pocket we pick up fourteen head with nary a scratch. Two old cows (each twelve-plus years, which is old for a cow) and a bunch of young stock. These old ladies knew where to hide! Wisdom from days gone by.

After a long day, we have thirty-two alive and loaded. Some might not make it, but we have to bring them home to give them a chance. They have made it this far. More jarring, though, is to walk down the drainage by the old Mountain House Ridge corral and to find twenty-six dead cattle, spread from top to bottom. That fetid smell of death permeates the walk I used to love.

Even after finding the dead cattle on Hartman Bar Ridge, I wonder why we found more than half of them alive, unlike anywhere else. If anything, I had assumed that this steep ridge would give them no chance at all. Then I realize that there had been a much smaller fire here about five years earlier. The countryside is more open now, and so the new fire had moved through quickly. Less fuel, so more things lived. Trees, wildlife, and cows.

I would later observe the same phenomenon in the remnants of the town of Feather Falls, where only a school and cemetery remain. The school had more than eighty students less than fifty years ago, until the lumber mill closed and the village died. The Bear Fire, I would discover, destroyed the school. The cemetery, however, still stands with green, stately pines respecting the graves of mostly Native American veterans, whose plots each have a flag. Family members maintain the cemetery, keeping it free of deadfall and litter. All the trees live.

Day five begins.

We move as fast as we can, opening roads with saws and running four-wheelers down every logging spur. We hope against hope to find more cow tracks, but there are none. Hartman Bar Ridge is about ten miles long with the only narrow, paved, Forest Service road in the entire mountain range. Nothing new but the cow tracks we found yesterday. Nothing at Socrates Spring, Harry Waite's, the Lower Reservoir, DeJonah,

Sheep Tank Meadow, Stag Point, Steward Ravine—or at a hundred more named places that are being lost. Nothing.

Up by Tamarack Flat, I run into five pickups belonging to timber reps from Sierra Pacific, the private landholder whom we lease from and who has private property throughout our range. I am walking the logging road, looking and listening, because I ran out of gas a mile or so from here. Too much country to cover! They are no doubt shocked to see me in that desolation, striding down the road, covered in ash from head to foot. I know most of them. Foresters by trade who, like me, love the land. "It is all gone," they say. Almost. I tell them I can show them a few pockets where trees survive. But very few. We are sad and angry together.

By the end of a grueling day, we have seven head loaded. Five of them are cattle we have seen before and were just able to get portable panels to and load. Three of them are badly burned and will get a chance to eat and drink before they most likely die or need to be euthanized. We know of three more live cattle whom we have seen and not loaded. That may be it. More than one hundred brought home, but I will be surprised if eighty manage to remain alive. Many of those who live will have lost their baby calves to fire. There are no words. Twenty percent of the herd we drove to the mountains on June 1. Maybe.

Our day-six crew is smaller. Rob has flown back to his duty station in the army. Kate has gone back to her work as a veterinarian. They left with overwhelming sadness and promised, "We will help any way we can." Most of the rest of our crew had to get back to their jobs too but "are a phone call away with a stock trailer" if we find something to load and need help beyond the two trailers we will haul ourselves. I doubt we will. Kyle and I start the search again, compulsively walking creeks and canyons that we have already searched, hoping something straggles in from behind. You never know and you can't quit. That is not who we are.

And now we go on. What will happen? This is devastating, emotionally and financially. And I am not sure of the next steps. I do know this: We must change our land-management practices if we expect the West to survive. It is best done locally, not from D.C. or Sacramento, but I have tilted at windmills before.

We won't quit. We need to get tougher and stronger. We never have quit for 140 years, and I won't be the first. Suffer the bureaucratic maze and try to make incremental change. And, as always, work with nature. I have to. Juni Daley and the next generation need to see the mountains the same way we have seen them forever, to have hot chocolate on a cold fall morning, and to gather cows. It can't be just stories from her grandad.

We find an orphan heifer calf today, about two weeks old. Her mother didn't make it. Kyle stumbles on her hiding spot in one of the few living willow patches along a stream. He follows her for over an hour, straight up from the bottom of a canyon. We catch her and then put her on a bottle of milk replacer. This rescue is good for my heart. My granddaughter Juni's first heifer, I decide! They can grow up together.

We see life at Fall River today. Green grass trying to sprout by a spring. Life is resilient. So are we. Next year. And the next one hundred.

POSTSCRIPT

It is day twelve, and we are still working at the same pace because we have no choice. We are finding one or two live cows per day, so it is difficult to stop, but the dwindling number means we have to shift our focus to those who live. It is hard to do. We have put twelve hundred miles on the four-wheelers on old logging roads and skid trails in the last few days. I quit counting the number of tires we have ruined and how much chainsaw work we have been doing.

Unfortunately, we have had to begin euthanizing some of the cattle whom we brought home. But they were home for a while, fed and watered.

The fire is still not contained and takes runs depending on the wind. I am not sure what next year will bring. [Editor's note: The Bear Fire started on September 8, 2020, and it was finally contained on December 14, 2020.]

Long-term Stewardship in a Short-term World

Dan Macon

My two favorite farmer-authors, Wendell Berry and James Rebanks, often write about the agrarian importance of long-term attachment to place. Kentuckian Berry is part of a farming community that has existed for centuries. Rebanks, who is from England, raises sheep on pastures that have known his family's livestock for much longer than that. Both eloquently describe the commitment to and knowledge of the land that comes from this multigenerational tenure.

As a Californian, and as a rancher in whom the ranching gene lay dormant for several generations, I sometimes find myself envious of the ties that farmers like Berry and Rebanks have to their places. Sometimes I feel that no matter how carefully I ranch or how observantly I watch the world around me, I'll never know the places where my sheep graze as intimately as someone whose family has been on the land for centuries. And yet, as I watch some of the successful first-generation farmers and ranchers in my community—and as I watch my own ranching endeavors—I'm hopeful that careful and observant farming can lead to this deep-rooted knowledge of place here in the foothills of the Sierra Nevada.

For me, one of the great challenges to developing a durable commitment to the land in a place like Auburn is the economic value of the land itself. In California, as in much of the West, farming and ranching are often seen as interim land uses—ranchland is simply inventory for future development to a "higher and better" use (usually of houses). Because of this, real estate values typically outstrip the agricultural production value of the land. In simpler terms, farmers and ranchers can't afford to purchase land based on what it will grow. New farmers and ranchers (and fifteen years into my ranching career, I still consider myself a new rancher) typically must rent the land they farm.

Even with the most ironclad, long-term, written lease and the most supportive landlord, many ranchers (myself included) often have difficulty justifying long-term (and I mean multigenerational, long-term) thinking, given the insecure nature of our tenure on the land. Why should I invest time, money, and worry in land that someone else might own next week? Why should I invest if my landlord might lease the land to someone who offers more money next year?

For my part, I always try to take a longer-term view of my stewardship of other people's land, as well as my own. Based on conversations with other ranchers and on observations of their management, I think most of us do. Despite the often-thin economic returns from grazing livestock, most of us are motivated as much by our love of the land and of our animals as we are by economic reasons. For me, the work is too hard, and the risks are too great to continue to ranch without this long-term commitment to stewardship—even on land that I know I may not be able to graze next year.

However, sometimes our long-term goals can conflict with the short-term needs of our landlords, and reducing wildfire danger is just one such example. Some of the landowners for whom we graze would prefer that we graze off all the annual vegetation before fire season starts in June. While fire hazard is a consideration in our management planning, we're also concerned about having enough dry forage to return to in the fall. We look at this dry grass as a standing hay crop, not just as a potential fire threat. To address these conflicting objectives, we prioritize our summer grazing to protect homes while reserving other areas for fall grazing.

We seem to be living in an era that emphasizes immediate gratification, which makes farming and ranching all the more unusual. The decisions I made last fall about which rams to put with which ewes will influence the genetic makeup and quality of my flock for the rest of my ranching life. Similarly, our management decisions about how long to graze an area, how long to rest pastures, and when to use specific pieces of land—in other words, our entire approach to grazing management—will influence the quality of our grazing land next fall, next year, and for many years to come.

To make these decisions, a rancher must know his or her livestock and landscapes intimately. These are complex natural, social, and economic systems, and operationally specific knowledge only comes with years of careful observation and recordkeeping on the part of the rancher. I'm often reminded that I won't always get these decisions right, but because I ranch for the long term, I'll have another chance to try. And livestock must know the land as well as the rancher. Our sheep know the landscapes that they graze: having watched generations of our ewes graze the same lands for more than a decade now (a blink of the eye to someone like James Rebanks), I realize that they have spatial and temporal memories, just as I do.

As I consider our changing climate, I believe that farmers and ranchers are crucial agents of adaptation. We deal with changes—on the land, in the environment, in the weather, in the market—on a daily, weekly, and annual basis. When our conversations move beyond the politics of climate change, I am always struck by the creativity and intensity that farmers and ranchers bring to our discussions of adaptation. Long-term stewardship, I think, even in the face of uncertain tenure on the land, requires us to constantly adapt. The practical, problem-solving focus of farmers and ranchers is critical to our future, well beyond the fact that all of us need to eat.

Our small-scale sheep operation won't solve the world's problems (climatic or otherwise). That said, we're blessed at the moment with landlords who appreciate and share our long-term focus and commitment to their land. And this gives me great hope: the fact that there are others in our community who value long-term stewardship suggests that we might move beyond our society's short-term focus.

Predators

Kathy DeForest

It's a sunny, twenty-eight-degree, January morning in 2020. This is usually the kind of day in Modoc County, California, when I enjoy the natural beauty that surrounds me on our ranch. Tom and I quietly follow three open (nonpregnant) cows up the wooden alley to load them into our stock trailer, and we close the gate behind them.

For forty-nine years, as husband and wife and ranching partners, we've strived to improve the productivity and quality of our cattle. We feed them well, keep them healthy, and provide protection. An old timer once told us: "I take care of my cows. They take care of me." That is how it is. It's not just stewardship. It is a mutual dependency.

In order to remain financially sustainable, we need to make some sacrifices. It is the policy of our small mom-and-pop cattle ranch to send to market any cows that are not producing calves and are no longer helping to pay the bills. Every time we send a cow "down the road," we silently say a prayer of gratitude for what she has done for us in this circle of life. She may not have provided us great financial riches, but she has enabled us to do what we love, while providing tasty, healthy food and beef byproducts for our country and beyond. And she has enabled us to maintain and improve our environment through water, wildlife, soil, and vegetation conservation practices.

This particular morning is more difficult than many others. Tears run down my face as I say goodbye to cow #301. She is one of our registered Hereford cows and has raised four mighty fine bulls and one heifer in her seven years. Although #301 was never formally trained nor halter broken, she has always been gentle. Unlike every other cow in our herd, she allows us to come up to her to pet and scratch her. In fact, she comes to us for attention.

Our veterinarian checked #301 in November along with some other cows. She was pregnant at that time. But one day in December, at feeding time, I saw the telltale sign of abortion from the string of organic matter and mucus hanging out of her. I was heartbroken.

Now I must regretfully say goodbye to her. She did everything she could for us, and with a personality to boot. She raised good calves. She was easy to handle. She was pretty to look at. I am so tempted to tell Tom not to load her into the trailer. Oh, I am tempted! But, as the one who does the bookkeeping and banking, I know that we cannot afford to keep a 1,550-pound pet. We must be careful and diligent about our finances. And that is not always easy. Nor is it easy to say farewell to the animals in our care.

As Tom drives away with the cows in the trailer, I have a moment to think. I know that we have devoted our lives to the well-being of that cow and to the rest of our herd. We strive to provide a high quality of life for them while they are in our care. And I know that when she walks down that final loading ramp, she will meet her demise instantly and painlessly, never knowing what happened. That is a compassionate blessing.

My thoughts turn to other livestock and wildlife that aren't as fortunate as #301. At least she did not have to endure an agonizing death from a predator. Of the various predators in California, including domestic dog packs, cougars, bears, and coyotes, wolves are at the forefront of my mind.

I became involved with this issue when the famous, male, gray wolf, OR-7 (the first confirmed wild wolf in California since 1924), gallivanted through the state in 2011 and 2012. At that time gray wolves were protected under the U.S. Endangered Species Act. I could not fathom how the government could tell me that I was not allowed to protect my livestock from a predator like a wolf. After all, I knew from personal experience in 1970 how a pack of dogs could wipe out a flock of registered Suffolk ewes in one night. Those ewes had been my 4-H and FFA project, one that had been putting me through college. How on earth could we now accept packs of wolves?

Since then, I have reached out, learned a lot, and hoped that I could make a difference. I have written to and spoken publicly and privately with various nongovernmental organizations, as well as with the California Fish and Game Commission, state and federal wildlife agencies and officials, government trappers, ranchers, legal-defense teams, politicians, and anyone else willing to communicate with me. Tom and I have hosted tours of our ranch and the surrounding Modoc National Forest. We have always explained why ranchers are so protective and passionate about the safety of their livestock and why we try to learn from others about how we can survive predators. Has all this communicating helped? At this stage of the game, I feel the answer is "No," but I am not giving up hope.

Things got real in 2014 when the California Fish and Game Commission listed the gray wolf as an endangered species under the California Endangered Species Act (CESA). The commission is the governing body that sets rules and regulations for the California Department of Fish and Wildlife (CDFW). The commission did this without respect for CDFW's own recommendation to refrain from listing gray wolves as endangered. Nor did they consider the pleas from hunters, ranchers, and other concerned citizens regarding the harmful impact wolves would have on other wildlife and livestock. In my opinion, the commission, appointed by the governor and pushed by wolf advocacy groups, made a political decision regarding wildlife. So be it.

I can understand how this debacle happened. California, like much of the rest of the United States, is now populated by people who are generations removed from the land. These people want to do the right thing. I predict that I would be the same way if I lived in the city and had never had the experiences in life that I have had. My love for animals, just like that of many wolf lovers, is an innate characteristic of good people. Therefore, many people are caught up in the fairy tale and propaganda told by wolf-advocacy groups. Ironically, these same people who want to do the right thing do not take into account their own personal contributions to the urbanization, overpopulation, and infrastructure that have fragmented the state. Compare California as it is today with what it was like one hundred years ago, when the last known wolf was killed. It is a drastically different place.

Ranchers are caught in the middle of this wildlife renaissance. They are told, "Just use nonlethal methods to protect your livestock," such as fladry (hanging colored flags on a line or rope), horns, lights, and guard dogs. These have only proven to be short-term remedies, however. Wolves quickly become accustomed to these Band-Aid fixes and ignore them. Guard dogs sometimes work, but several courageous dogs have been killed or maimed in the process. Range riders may be effective when they are present, but they can't be with livestock 24–7, and hiring them is prohibitively expensive for small ranches. Range riders are also not feasible in open-range situations, such as on the Modoc plateau, where cattle spread out in many small groups to graze the small, hidden "stringer meadows" nestled in the vast, rugged, high-desert country. There is no easy answer for protection of livestock in wolf country.

There have been discussions about compensation programs for California ranchers in response to predator losses. There are many different opinions in the ranch community regarding this. For me personally, there is no money that can cover the loss, not to mention the anguish endured. How does one compensate for years of investing in genetic and behavioral improvements for livestock that can be lost overnight to a predator?

In 2020, according to the California Fish and Wildlife website, there were seven confirmed cattle killed by wolves in Lassen, Plumas, and Modoc Counties. These included small calves, six-hundred- to seven-hundred-pound calves, and full-grown cows. Reports of these kills were based on subcutaneous and muscular hemorrhages in the legs, hind ends, and necks; hemorrhages indicating that bites in the carcasses occurred while the animals were alive; and disturbed vegetation and forest debris showing evidence of struggles. This indicates to me that the victims experienced a slow, tortuous death by the wolf pack. And there are more kills that are never found.

In early January 2021, the CDFW website named the Lassen Pack as the only known, established one in the state. This pack apparently comprises an alpha male, two producing females, and their various offspring. Fast-forward to March 1, 2024, and according to the CDFW website, there are now seven established wolf packs in California. It also reports that there were thirty-five confirmed livestock depredations by wolves in 2023. A CDFW wolf compensation program was implemented but is already reportedly running out of funds.

In the meantime (knock on wood), Tom and I have not had any depredations from wolves. But we feel bad for the ranchers who have not been so lucky with their livestock.

Please don't get me wrong. I appreciate all of God's creatures, great and small. Wolves, I am the first to admit, are magnificent animals. They should never be completely exterminated. However, at times they can become problematic, especially in settled, populated regions like California. Here they do not have room to roam and to live in a dynamic, healthy habitat. Contrast California's size, infrastructure, and human population with Canada's vast remoteness and much smaller number of people. If you were a wolf, where would you want to live? I'd take Canada, the gray wolf's original habitat. The wolves we have in California today are descendants of those from the original experiment that transplanted Canadian gray wolves to Yellowstone and to parts of Idaho in 1995. I believe the lucky wolves are the ones still in Canada.

But here we are today, where wolves are better protected legally than livestock. Since the 2014 listing under CESA, no one may "hunt, pursue, harass, capture, or kill" a gray wolf. This includes a wolf caught in the act of harming or killing livestock. I find that outrageous! I am a grandmother who has never gotten a parking ticket. But if I protect my cattle from harm by shooting a wolf caught in the act of trying to kill them, I can be imprisoned and fined. It would be unbearable for me to witness a wolf pack harassing and torturing my cattle and not be able legally to do one darn thing about it. To this day, I thank God that I have not been put in this situation. And I empathize with those who have.

I must gratefully acknowledge that as of January 2021, gray wolves are no longer listed as endangered under the federal Endangered Species Act. Yet they remain completely protected under California law.

What is my solution for the wolf predicament throughout the state of California? Sadly, I don't have any short-term answers. However, in the long term, there are things that we could and should work on. I hope that all of agriculture can come together to create an extensive, long-term campaign to educate the general public about the wonderful things that agriculture does for our environment and society; and, through such a campaign, that the general public will again be persuaded to allow farmers and ranchers to deal legally with problem wolves (and other predators) that cause harm to their livestock. It is time we tell our story.

On our ranch, Tom and I will continue to take the best care we possibly can of our cattle. We'll keep them healthy and vibrant. We will be open to learning more about wolf and cattle behavior. We will continue to communicate with people who are willing to respectfully share ideas and to communicate about wolves and livestock interactions. And we will not give up.

So yes, #301, you lived a good life. I remain grateful for you. And I pray that as long as Tom and I are physically able to, we will continue to care for your offspring and herd mates. They, like you, deserve the best quality of life that we can provide.

Thank God

Mike Williams

I led my horse from the corral
Full of worry and stress
I was wondering how things
Could be such a mess

One thing that had me
Somewhat concerned
The loan payment due
Was more than I'd earned

Expenses were higher
And profits were lower
Stretching nickels to dimes
Was making me older

Another thing on my mind
Was the drought
Whether or not I'd survive it
Was somewhat in doubt

The best springs that I had
Were no more than seeps
And there wasn't much water
Left in the creek

The grass that was left
Was disappearing fast
And I wasn't sure
Just how long it would last

As I saddled my horse
My mood damp as the dew
I had no idea what
I was going to do

But as I stepped in the stirrup
And climbed up in the saddle
All of my stresses
Began to unravel

As I rode out I started
To relax a bit
I startled some deer
Down by the creek

Topped out on a ridge
To a beautiful sky
Heard the screech of a hawk
As it soared way up high

I rode through the cattle
Some lounging some grazing
I checked out the calves
Some nursing some playing

I was so overwhelmed
With the peace and the love
That God seemed to be sharing
With me from above

I stepped down off my horse
And bent down on one knee
I thanked God for the blessing
He'd given me

I still had my worries
Wasn't sure how I'd get through it
But I had to thank God
I was able to do it

Summers in a National Forest Service Lease

Kayla Delbar Moore

It is quite normal for summer mornings to start at around 4 AM in this house. I am not an early bird and never have been, but I dislike the heat later in the day. Those two things together tell you that I really shouldn't live in Potter Valley, California, during the summer. It is hot, and the water from flood irrigation, paired with a lack of wind, creates a southern-U.S.-style humidity. I tell you this because almost every summer that I can recall, my family has turned our cows out on U.S. Forest Service land in Upper Lake.

If we streamline our adventure of heading to the forest by already having food prepped and horses in the corral, it still takes us almost three hours to get from our house to the top of Elk Mountain Road. We also must take into consideration which trailer, horses, and dog pair we are going to take on any given day. Moola, my dun mare, isn't quite fond of the slatted floors in the pipe trailer, but Abby, my mom's mare, loves to make a ruckus in the Wilson. We also need to decide what the goal is for the day. Are we checking, loading, or exploring? Then the real question: Do we need the panels and the whole dog gang?

During the early morning routine, we catch the horses via the limited light of a headlamp or, nowadays, a cell phone flashlight. We saddle them with the help of these lights and get wiped out by the excited cow dogs at least three times before we get the ponies loaded. Once I hear the click-clack of hooves against the stock trailer floor, I know it is time to load the dogs. We clip the dogs in—except for Pearl, because in the mornings, her highness gets to travel on top of the stack of leather chinks, bridles, sweaters, and water bottles in the back seat—and we triple-check that we have enough water. Now we are ready to go, and I will nap in the back seat until I am rudely awakened by the incline as we begin to crawl up the face of Elk Mountain.

These days, Elk Mountain Road consists of crater after crater of broken asphalt. Big rigs, dozers, campers, and more travel this road every summer, and it just keeps breaking up. Thank goodness it hasn't flattened one of our trailer tires when we're fully loaded. As we scale the switch-backs and play "dodge the potholes," I start scanning the landscape. Since the August 2018 Ranch Fire, we've been able to see straight through the burnt timber and manzanita. The cows begin to dot the hillside as we get higher and higher up. Our goal is not to move these gals, who seem fine, until late June and to check some other trails instead.

Our U.S. Forest Service summer lease in the Mendocino National Forest is about thirty-thousand acres of mountains and ravines where we run one hundred sixty head of cattle from May to November. This place gives *open range* great meaning, as the cows can nap in the middle of the paved county road or wander into a private landowner's yard. Our cows love it here, some so much so that we have a hard time tracking them down to bring them home in the fall.

Every day that we come out here is an adventure that allows us to live the true meaning of the get-outside movement. I love to unload my horse, unclip the dogs, step in the saddle, and hit the closest bike trail, then veer off on that brushed-up cow trail that leads from ridgeline to ridgeline. We track water, feed, and cow sign all day to find the small group of cows—ones that will calve in the fall—that we saw eating along-side the spring we crossed right before we unloaded. The beauty of this place is that on some days, the whole mountain is empty, not a deer, dirt bike, or cow in sight. Then, the next day, we're trotting up the pave-ment behind that lead cow, while bikes are coming in off the trail and campers are idling behind us. The best feeling, though, is quietly push-ing cows down the road through a campsite on a busy weekend. Families get excited, kids' mouths drop open, the dogs show off a little, and the horses put a little extra pep in their step.

The worst feeling is finding a poisoned cow dead at a water hole or following an old cow trail right to an illegal marijuana grow that spooks my horse. Public lands create so many opportunities for my family and others to respectfully utilize and enjoy the outdoors, but not everyone respects our lands or the wildlife that call them home. I wouldn't say I often feel unsafe riding in the National Forest, but I definitely won't visit some places alone. There are trails that used to be roads that are now cut open just for foot traffic. There are creeks and springs littered with trash, where the Forest Service workers will not go. There are once-beautiful cabins and ponds now turned into drying sheds and swamps. This piece of mountain ground is slowly being destroyed by illegal use, lack of logging, lack of resources, and lack of management.

On some days I feel a bit cowboy-ish as we sit in our saddles all day, cutting out brush, crossing washed-out roads, and tracking the dogs' barking from miles away. On other days I feel like a range warrior as I cross property boundaries during harvesttime, trying to bring home those last twenty cows.

We have experienced drought and thick feed years, fire and summer storms, friendly campers and bikers, angry and welcoming landowners. I have become part of a unique group of people who frequent this place because they just want to be left alone. I grew the most in this community of hermits at a time when we were all worried about coming home alive in the summer of 2018, as the Ranch Fire tore through homes and honey holes. We all cared about saving what was dear to us. For me it was my cows, the one hundred momma cows I had sent to the summer lease. They were the breeding heifers that I had promised to protect, but I only found them three months after the fire, starving and barely able to feed their own babies.

Spending time in our Forest-Service summer lease has brought me to my highest highs, while the new and growing obstacles have brought me to my lowest lows. For years, my family and the families before us have provided a service to this community, protecting the rangeland from overgrowth by grazing our cattle. We have pushed for better roads, logging, and both environmental and personal protections so that everyone can enjoy this forest. We spend all our resources to benefit everyone's adventures in this mountain range. It should be important—not only to us but to everyone—that we continue to graze, log, and enjoy the national forests so that we keep them alive with all kinds of wildlife and creatures. It is our opportunity to continue to learn and to provide for the land.

My Ranching Story

KAYLA DELBAR MOORE

There I was, walking into my elementary PE class and carrying a note about how I needed a break from running. I didn't enjoy running, but why did I need a signed excuse on this particular Monday? Well, because on Sunday, like every weekend in the summer, I had gone with my mom and our cowhand to gather cows and bring them home from the summer lease. This was my life: I woke up in the pickup in the middle of nowhere, and I rode my horse, begged for snacks, and daydreamed. We moved cows, gathered cows, loaded cows, and took them back to the ranch for the winter.

That Sunday, an uncooperative cow and I had a disagreement, or, as my dad's note explained it, we "played football." You guessed right: I lost. As my mom and the cowhand were loading this cow, I got out of the pickup to "help." I am sure there was a reason why I was in the pickup, but helping was not it. That is when my mom had me "block the hole" to get this angry momma in the trailer (I am pretty sure that this is the lineman's position in football). Feet firmly planted on the ground, I wasn't going to move. When that cow took one look at me, I did just that: I did not move. One cow and twelve dogs went right over the top of me, and there I lay, back in the dirt with tears on my face. I gimped around school with a bruised foot that showed I was not a very good football player, but you can bet that I was proud of that bruise.

I grew up with bruises like that, and I was proud of most of them. There was one day when I came off two horses at a branding and almost refused to get on the third. Luckily for me, ole Buck really just wanted to sit at the fence and not move. Then there was a day when my hoodie caught on a branch, and my roan mare hung me up in that tree. All those moments were part of a carefree childhood, when I got to roam on old ranch mares through the mountains with my best friend, hunting for cows, dreaming of music, and talking about how we would escape a bear attack. We got to camp in the mountains and to ride on the hay truck in the pastures. The experiences we lived are ones that I wish every kid could have, as they shaped me into who I am today.

Those experiences have created a passion in me to preserve ranching, farming, and outdoor activities. They also drove me to get a degree in agriculture. Those and the fact that I had at first wanted to be a veterinarian. After realizing that microbiology and I were not friends, however, I took a step back and realized that what I really wanted was to raise cattle. I wanted those childhood experiences back. The family ranch couldn't pay me to do what I wanted to do. I didn't have a lease of my own, so the next best thing would be to work for someone else.

When I had finished college, I set out to find a career. After enduring many "you just aren't what we are looking for" conversations, I was offered a new type of internship with GENEX Beef. It was one of the best things that could have happened to me. I set out for southern Colorado in January and, thankfully, encountered one of the quietest winters they had seen. I had grown up running one hundred head of momma cows at a seven-hundred-foot elevation on a multigenerational family ranch, and now I worked with two thousand head of mostly registered momma cows at seven thousand feet and on a one-generation ranch with multiple employees. What I learned over those two months went far beyond calving and doctoring pink eye and well into lease agreements and employee management. I learned how to treat people so that they become like family. I learned how to enjoy life, grow my passion, and earn a community's respect.

These were lessons that could take me beyond just one cattle operation. After calving out most of the cows during the internship, I was able to become certified in artificial insemination. This experience felt like I polished my boots and put silver on my spurs. I was proud of myself, but just as I was accomplishing all this, I found out that my mom was being airlifted to the hospital with a broken leg.

Mom was trying to run the ranch, work a full-time job, and raise my brothers. And I was away when her mare practiced her floor routine, somersaulting while moving down a hill after some cows. As she flipped, the saddle snapped both bones in my mom's leg. Thankfully my father wasn't too far behind Mom, and the helicopter was able to retrieve her.

I was in a hard place: Should I go home and care for my mother and the cows, only to lose out on my internship opportunity, or should I stay and be of no help to the family?

Long story short, my family survived without me, and I completed an incredible internship. I had the opportunity to travel from northeast Oregon to central New Mexico and eastern Nebraska. I visited small towns, large and small cattle operations, and made lots of friends. I learned new skills and discovered that bunkhouse cooks are the best kind of people. I learned that you always take care of the maintenance guys and feed truck drivers and that breakfast burritos with green chili sauce hit the sweet spot.

After my journey, I was offered my dream job. I began to work on a registered Angus ranch in eastern Oregon. I got to live away from people with my dog and horses. I spent my days checking cows, learning to drive the semi, and becoming more in check with who I am. I had big dreams and great plans. I had ambitious goals and slept hard. I fought the local mouse population in my cabin and fell in love with checking fence lines. I learned how to "farmer" the cows—putting hay on my pickup's bed and having the cows follow me—to save my horse a few more miles. I learned that I wasn't always meant to be somewhere at a given time. I learned that sometimes you have to fight for who you are and what you know. I learned that not every good idea is welcome. My dream and someone else's dream are not the same, and that is okay. But I had to learn that the hard way.

I was trying to be a successful, female ranch hand, but I wasn't the best roper; I didn't wear the right hat or look the way others thought I should. Maybe I needed to get off the ranch more than once a month for people to meet me. Maybe my views were too worldly. But then suddenly, none of this mattered: forces took me home.

They took me home to a place that was comfortable but where many people saw me as the young kid who never took anything seriously except for her friendships. Where I couldn't pursue my dreams without a paying job.

So, I went back to school to chase my passion for learning, teaching, and agriculture. It was then I realized that it was now or never to start my own cattle herd. I bought ten fancy Angus cows with their calves, and they started out with a bit of a spicy temperament. I fought with these ladies and almost lost the relationship with the man I love because they just wouldn't calm down. Many fence lines and years later, these ladies will just about eat out of my hand. The ten head have grown to twenty-two, and my small lease has become two large leases that I manage.

What changed over the four years between purchasing the original mommas and managing them today? My confidence in myself, confidence in my personal relationship, a paycheck, and my passion for my cows. I have grown. I have taken action by letting people see that I am not that nerdy kid anymore. I can rope, ride, and track cows like I have done my entire life. I have a long way to go, but I know that I am setting a precedent, just like my mom did, showing that women can have a voice in ranching. Women can handle themselves, can be strong and stable in their dreams and goals. This is the legacy that I want to create: women in ranching and women having a voice in multigenerational ranching.

Acknowledgments

We worked as a team on this collection of essays and poems. Susan Edinger Marshall and Dan Macon had a dream to pull this collection together. Michael Delbar of the California Rangeland Trust and Valerie Elder of The Buckeye reached out to ranching families throughout the state, as did Dan Macon of the University of California Cooperative Extension. Grant Scott-Goforth, of Cal Poly Humboldt's Marketing and Communications (CPH MARCOM), helped with the editing and wrote the introductions to the sections: "Roots," "Transitions," and "Resilience." We were determined to preserve the authentic voices of the contributors. Connie Webb, also a former member of the fabulous CPH MARCOM team, prepared the map. Thanks also to Kacie Flynn of Cal Poly Humboldt's Sponsored Programs Foundation, who provided financial support. Most of all, we thank the diverse contributors who shared very personal stories, poems, and family histories to make this collection possible. Royalties generated by sales of this book will be divided between the California Rangeland Trust to conserve rangelands and the Cal Poly Humboldt Steven E. Slusser Memorial Endowment to support range and soils students for field trips, competitions, and participation in professional meetings.

Contributors

MIA ARTADI DIGIOVANNI and BIANCA ARTADI SHAPERO are the eldest granddaughters of Raymond and Teresa Talbott. As they were growing up, they spent countless hours driving around with their grandparents, windows down, cigarette smoke and dust billowing in, listening to stories about their Basque heritage, their family, and raising sheep, hearing priceless stories and memories that they want to preserve for years to come. Mia attended the University of San Diego and has a master's in health-care administration from the University of Southern California. Bianca attended the University of California, Davis, and now works as the project manager for Star Creek Land Stewards Inc. alongside her mother. She also contributes to the management of Talbott Sheep Co.

HEATHER BERNIKOFF (YO'EME/YAQUI) is an Indigenous land steward. Her education and training are in community health, and with this knowledge, she has engaged in actions and advocated for policies that improve the health of land, air, water, and all living things. Heather served as a planning commissioner in Mariposa County and received a gubernatorial appointment to the Sierra Nevada Conservancy Board in 2021. She loves the *huya ania* ("wilderness world") and continues to play in the mud with her dogs, plant seeds, and live in reciprocity with the land, along with her husband, on their ranch in the Sierra Nevada foothills.

GLORIA COTTRELL was born in Fortuna, California, in 1939. She married Graham Cottrell in 1958, moved to the Cottrell Ranch in Bridgeville, and started the Three Rivers Logging Co. Though she is still participating in some of the day-to-day activities on the ranch, she takes the most pleasure in instilling a love for the property in her grandson, who is the fifth generation to live and work on the ranch.

DAVID A. DALEY is a fifth-generation, Butte County, commercial cattle producer, who runs the family ranch near Oroville alongside his son Kyle. Daley's family has had cattle on U.S.-Forest-Service grazing permits in the Plumas National Forest for generations, making him well versed in the issues public-land ranchers face and passionate about preserving public-land grazing. Daley is at the forefront of California's beef industry, holding leadership positions on the local, state, and national levels. He recently served as the Associate Dean of the College of Agriculture at California State University, Chico, and was an animal science professor at the university for many years.

KATHY DEFOREST is a cattle rancher in Modoc County, California. She and her husband, Tom, worked for several large and small ranches in Northern California and Southeastern Oregon before going into the cattle business on their own in 1997. They have two daughters and two grandchildren. Kathy studied animal science at Cal Poly, San Luis Obispo, and at Yuba Junior College, Marysville, California. She is a past president of the Fall River Big Valley Cattlemen's Association, a member of the California Cattlemen's Association, and a director on the Modoc County Grazing Advisory Committee. Kathy and Tom received the 2018 Excellence in Range Management Award from the California-Pacific section of the Society of Range Management.

PAMELA GOFORTH DOIRON is a California native who grew up in a small, agricultural community, and, after earning an English degree from Santa Clara University, spent too many years working in Silicon Valley. Fortunately, she escaped and returned to rural life in a remote corner of Santa Barbara County. She and her family operate a cattle ranch where land conservation and soil restoration go hand in hand with livestock production. Writing is second nature: she produced her first poem at age seven and hasn't stopped since.

VALERIE ELDER is the former Executive Director of The Buckeye Conservancy and a Professor of Forestry at College of the Redwoods in Eureka, California. She spent several years working with forest landowners, ranchers, farmers, and foresters with the University Extension Service in West Virginia, California, and Oregon. Her family manages a logging business, forest, and small herd of cattle in Kneeland. She studied forestry at Cal Poly, San Luis Obispo, and earned an MS from West Virginia University.

WALT GIACOMINI is a retired Humboldt County, California, rancher. He graduated from Cal Poly, San Luis Obispo, in 1964, and he worked on Northern California ranches and on a research farm in Davis, California. In the late seventies he taught farm management and coached rodeo at Blue Mountain Community College in Pendleton, Oregon. In 1980 he moved back to Humboldt County, where he managed, and later operated, ranches at Salmon Creek and on the Bear River.

DICK GIBFORD lives in an isolated cow camp on the edge of the San Rafael Wilderness about ten miles southwest of Cuyama Valley, California. He has made a living most all his life "a-horseback," cowboying for one outfit or another. These days he stays put where he's at, riding and looking after the cattle for the Walking R Ranch, the oldest cow outfit still going in this part of the country.

DAN MACON is a first-generation shepherd in the Sierra Nevada foothills near Auburn, California, producing meat, wool, and targeted grazing services. He is also a livestock and natural resources advisor for the University of California Cooperative Extension. Previously, Dan was the founding executive director of the California Rangeland Trust, a statewide organization devoted to conserving working ranches. Dan holds a BS in agricultural economics from UC Davis and a master of agriculture degree in integrated resource management from Colorado State University.

SUSAN EDINGER MARSHALL is Professor Emerita of Rangeland Resources and Wildland Soils at Cal Poly, Humboldt. She has worked for the Cooperative Extension Service at the University of Arizona and for Purdue University in Indiana. She earned a BS in environmental science and a PhD in soil science at UC Riverside and an MS in range management at the University of Arizona.

DINA MOORE partners with her husband, Mark, daughters Lauren and Teal, their spouses, and her grandchildren at the Lone Star Ranch, a cattle-ranching operation that spans seven generations. She is a board member of the Humboldt Area Foundation, and she is an adviser to the North Coast Regional Land Trust. She has also served on the North Coast

Regional Water Quality Control Board. Dina attended UC Davis, and she is a California Ag Leadership alumna. In 2015 Lone Star Ranch received the Society for Range Management's Excellence in Range Management Award for North America and the Leopold Conservation Award in 2016.

KAYLA DELBAR MOORE is an agriculture teacher at Potter Valley High School and a cattle rancher in Mendocino and Lake Counties. She earned her BS in animal science and communications at Washington State University. Kayla then used her knowledge from home and school to work on a seed-stock operation in Eastern Oregon. Today she balances her time among the family ranch, her own cattle operation, and the high school ag department.

MARILYN SAGEHORN RUSSELL is a third-generation rancher who owns and manages the Sagehorn-Russell Ranch, LLC—which her parents purchased in 1948 and where she grew up—in Mendocino County, California. She graduated from UC Berkeley in 1966 with a degree in zoology and taught field biology at Livermore High School for thirty-three years. She is devoted to the stewardship and conservation of open spaces and ranches. Her ranch is in a Conservation Easement with the California Rangeland Trust (CRT), and Marilyn and her husband, Jerry, received the Conservationist of the Year Award in 2019 from the CRT. Marilyn served on the Alameda County Resource Conservation Board for eight years and helped establish the Tri-Valley Trailblazers, a club devoted to horsemanship and trail riding that existed for fifty years. She currently serves on the advisory board for the Museum of Vertebrate Zoology at UC Berkeley. She loves to travel, especially on long-distance endurance horses, which she trained for many years. She has ridden on numerous historic trails throughout the West and as far away as Australia. Of course, her favorite rides involve herding cattle on the ranch and enjoying the land, which will be conserved as rangeland in perpetuity.

JESSICA SCHLEY is a writer, rider, and realtor in her hometown of Santa Ynez, California. She was raised on a multigenerational cattle ranch in the Happy Canyon area of Santa Barbara County, and although her family no longer holds the land, she is lucky to consider its new stewards dear friends. Jessica holds an interdisciplinary degree in land, policy, and representation in the West from UC Berkeley. She serves as the Chair of the California Rangeland Trust's Legacy Council, the largest land trust in the state, with over 306,000 acres permanently conserved to date. Their focus is on conserving rangelands and on helping to elevate the story of ranching and conservation.

PENELOPE (PENNY) SAMPERT SCRIBNER is a former elementary school principal and arts educator. As a UC Berkeley decorative arts graduate, Penny went on to receive her master's degree in school administration at Sacramento State University and spent her professional career working in elementary education. The daughter of a forester father, she values her time in the out-of-doors. Horse crazy from an early age, Penny was only six when she got her first one and has owned forty horses in her eighty years. She has spent her life combining her dedication to the arts, to the environment, to young people, and to the horses and dogs in her life.

LINDA STANSBERRY is a writer, rancher, and journalist from Northern California. She grew up on the Stansberry Ranch in Honeydew, California, leaving at age eighteen to earn a bachelor's degree in English from the University of San Francisco. She's spent the past twenty years writing novels, reporting on news in her hometown, traveling the world, and fixing fences.

JACK VARIAN is a cattle rancher and award-winning conservationist from the V6 Ranch in Parkfield, California. The son of an inventor and conservationist, Jack entered the ranching world in the late 1950s with a unique perspective. Over the sixty-plus years since then, Jack has managed the V6 Ranch along with his wife, Zee, and four generations of his family. Today the V6 Ranch sustains a cattle operation, agritourism, a hunting club, free-range chickens, and a newly planted pistachio orchard, all proudly managed by the family using holistic ranch-management techniques. In 2001 the Varian family placed a conservation easement on the V6 Ranch, protecting it as an open landscape in perpetuity.

LAUREN VARIAN is a third-generation rancher on the V6 Ranch. She lived in Ireland for seven years, working in the culture sector as a designer, producer, and content creator before returning to the ranch with her husband, Cian. Lauren now works on the ranch with her family, serving as the marketing manager and helping with day-to-day tasks in their cattle ranching, agritourism business, and conservation efforts. She and her husband also opened Middle Ridge Studio, a recording studio in a log cabin on the V6.

MIKE WILLIAMS is a rancher who runs Diamond W Cattle Company, a commercial cow/calf operation in Los Angeles County, along with his wife, Lynda. Mike has a deep love of ranching, enjoying both the lifestyle and working with the livestock. He is actively engaged in cattle industry efforts at the local, state, and national levels, working to preserve and promote ranching so that the lifestyle he has been blessed with can be enjoyed for generations to come.